In Action:
Improving Performance
in Organizations

American Society for Training & Development

IN ACTION

Improving Performance in Organizations

ELEVEN

CASE STUDIES

FROM THE

REAL WORLD

OF TRAINING

ASTD

JACK J. PHILLIPS
SERIES EDITOR

WILLIAM J. ROTHWELL

DAVID D. DUBOIS
EDITORS

Ordering information: Books published by the American Society for Training & Development can be ordered by calling 800.628.2783 or 703.683.8100.

Library of Congress Catalog Card Number: 98-74117
ISBN: 1-56286-100-X

Table of Contents

Introduction to the
In Action Series

A s are most professionals, the people involved in human resource
development (HRD) are eager to see practical applications of the
models, techniques, theories, strategies, and issues the field comprises. In recent years, practitioners have developed an intense desire
to learn about the success of other organizations when they implement
HRD programs. The Publishing Review Committee of the American Society for Training & Development has established this series of casebooks
to fill this need. Covering a variety of topics in HRD, the series should
add significantly to the current literature in the field.

This series has the following objectives:

- *To provide real-world examples of HRD program application and implementation.* Each case will describe significant issues, events, actions, and activities. When possible, the actual names of the organizations and individuals
involved will be used. In other cases, the names will be disguised, but
the events are factual.

- *To focus on challenging and difficult issues confronting the HRD field.* These
cases will explore areas where it is difficult to find information or where
the processes or techniques are not standardized or fully developed.
Also, emerging issues critical to success in the field will be covered in
the series.

- *To recognize the work of professionals in the HRD field by presenting best
practices.* Each book in the series will attempt to represent the most
effective examples in the field. The most respected organizations, practitioners, authors, researchers, and consultants will be asked to provide cases.

- *To serve as a self-teaching tool for people learning about the HRD field.* As a
stand-alone reference, each volume should be a very useful learning
tool. Each case will contain many issues and fully explore several topics.

- *To present a medium for teaching groups about the practical aspects of HRD.* Each
book should serve as a discussion guide to enhance learning
in formal and informal settings. Each case will have questions for

discussion. And each book will be useful as a supplement to general and specialized textbooks in HRD.

The topics for the volumes will be carefully selected to ensure that they represent important and timely issues in the HRD field. The editors for the individual volumes are experienced professionals in the field. The series will provide a high-quality product to fill a critical void in the literature. An ambitious schedule is planned.

If you have suggestions of ways to improve this series or an individual volume in the series, please respond directly to me. Your input is welcome.

Jack J. Phillips, Ph.D.
Series Editor
Performance Resources Organization
Box 380637
Birmingham, AL 35238-0637

Preface

In *Action* is a casebook series that focuses on important issues in human resource development (HRD), human performance improvement (HPI), and workplace learning and performance (WLP). To date, there have been more than 10 volumes in the series, focusing on such topics as measuring return-on-investment (two volumes), needs assessment, designing training programs, transfer of training, and learning organizations.

Target Audience

Improving Performance in Organizations should be of value to anyone who is interested in HPI, defined as "the systematic process of discovering and analyzing important human performance gaps, planning for future improvements in human performance, designing and developing cost-effective and ethically-justifiable interventions to close performance gaps, implementing the interventions, and evaluating the financial and nonfinancial results" in Rothwell's 1996 book *The ASTD Models for Human Performance Improvement: Roles, Competencies, and Outputs* (p. 79). HPI is about matching the right solutions to the right problems, about addressing causes by providing a range of solutions that may go beyond training and development, as Rothwell states in *Beyond Training and Development: State of the Art Strategies for Enhancing Human Performance,* published in 1996. It is also about going beyond traditional notions of work performance to include a competency-based approach, as Dubois makes clear in his 1993 book *Competency-Based Performance Improvement.*

The primary audience for this book is the practitioner who manages, coordinates, or oversees a full-service training department, training function, or training program that goes beyond merely offering training to identifying, solving, and anticipating human-performance problems. Those individuals are usually held accountable for achieving useful results—and are held responsible when they do not. For them, this volume shows how organizations of varied sizes and types have attempted to go beyond training to apply a broad range of HPI solutions to organizational needs.

The second audience for this book is the HRD practitioner who does not bear management or programmatic responsibility. These individuals are often the daily "shock troops" who undertake hand-to-hand combat, in the trenches, to identify and solve human performance problems or identify and seize human performance improvement opportunities. Like their management counterparts, they should understand HPI and be aware of when and how it may be applied. This volume provides a frame of reference for that purpose, showing by example how HPI can be carried out.

The third audience for this book is the researcher or academic who is looking for descriptions of how HRD practitioners are applying HPI in the real world so that they may supplement in-class HRD courses with a dose of HPI. Researchers and academics alike will find such cases in this volume.

The fourth and final audience for this book is the line manager. For a line manager, this book should illustrate when and how HPI may be applied to address real-world problems with human performance. The book raises, and addresses, many issues that should be considered when attempting to apply HPI.

The Cases

The cases in this volume represent a cross section of real-world efforts to apply a variety of performance improvement interventions. To find these cases, ASTD sought cases from their own members and from members of other organizations representing both practitioners and academics in the HR and HRD communities. It undertook multiple mailings to find authors. The volume editor also had over 100 phone calls made to recruit cases from well-known authors or well-known organizations.

The cases represented here reveal a broad range of views and approaches. The editors did not force authors to comply with some prescribed approach to HPI. Instead, the cases represent a range of efforts to go beyond training and development to improve performance in organizational settings.

Case Authors

The editors selected the case authors for the quality of the cases they submitted. Collectively, they represent a broad range of experience—from government, business, education, and nonprofit sectors. Most have had significant experience.

Best Practices?

The editors of this volume were determined to demonstrate that HRD practitioners can do more than just training. In fact, we often told prospective case authors that "we do not want cases about training as a performance improvement strategy, because enough has been written in other places about that. Tell us what you have done that improves performance but that goes beyond training."

As a result of this admonition and others, the cases in this book do not necessarily represent best-practice cases. Although some cases do embody best practices, most demonstrate the more typical, though realistic, struggles to apply HPI in real-world settings where other key stakeholders—such as line managers or senior executives—do not necessarily agree that such a role is appropriate for "trainers." These cases contain important lessons for HRD practitioners as they move beyond training to use a broad range of performance improvement strategies to address human performance improvement problems or to seize opportunities to improve human performance.

Acknowledgments

Any edited work of this kind necessarily demands the help—and support—of many people. Allow us first to express our appreciation to the case authors for their time, patience, and effort in preparing their cases. That required dedication to the profession that is beyond the norm.

Second, the editors wish to thank Jack Phillips, editor of the *In Action* series, for the patience he demonstrated as we struggled to find good cases and prepare them for publication. His assistant Patti Pulliam was most helpful throughout this process and deserves her own praise for her patience with volume editors as busy as we are. Special thanks also goes to Nancy Olson, vice president of publications at ASTD, for her extraordinary patience with this volume and its editors.

Third, we want to express our mutual appreciation to Dr. Rothwell's graduate research assistants Chris Howard and Daryl Hunt, who went above and beyond the call of duty to make over 100 long-distance phone calls on our behalf—using a script that we approved—to solicit case authors individually. Without that intense and short-term manuscript recruitment effort, this volume would not exist.

Dr. Rothwell also wishes to thank his wife, Marcelina, his daughter, Candice, his son, Froilan Perucho, and his daughter-in-law, Kristen Perucho, for their loving support during the time this book was assembled.

William J. Rothwell
State College, Pennsylvania
October 1998

David D. Dubois
Rockville, Maryland
October 1998

How to Use This Casebook

This book represents a broad cross section of efforts to link human resources development (HRD) with organizational strategy.

Using the Cases

This book can be used in several ways. It provides real-world cases demonstrating the efforts of HRD practitioners and consultants to link HRD with organizational strategy. Following are some of the possible ways to use the cases:

- HRD managers will find the cases excellent and thought-provoking examples of practical efforts to link HRD to organizational strategy.
- Academics and researchers will find a source of useful information about actual practices in the field as a base of comparison with theoretical descriptions. This book describes how it is really done, providing a counterpoint to what should be done.
- HRD students will find this book to be a useful supplement to college textbooks that provide theory but often do not provide sufficient descriptions of how those theories may fare when they are applied. Real cases demonstrating the difficulties inherent in application can enhance classroon discussion and provide a basis to discover, or test, theories.
- Line managers will find this book useful as they work with HRD practitioners to link HRD to organizational strategy. More specifically, understanding how other organizations have attempted the linkage of HRD and organizational strategy can provide a common language and basis for discussion and action.

Overview of the Case Studies

Figure 1 provides an overview of the case studies in this book. It lists the authors, cases, chapters in which they appear, industries, and type of human performance improvement effort made.

Figure 1. Overview of the case studies.

Author's Name	Case	Chapter Title	Industry	Type of HPI Effort
Dale C. Brandenburg	Danby Tool	Implementation of Workplace Education in a Small Manufacturing Company	Manufacturing	Training rewards
Jeremie Hill Grey Elizabeth A. Sharp Jennifer Fox Kennedy	Three-Five Systems, Inc.	Developing a Leadership Curriculum	Manufacturing	Performance support intervention
Marsha King	Alston Tanks	Improving Performance Through Competency-Based Selection Techniques	Manufacturing	Competency-based selection techniques
Danny Langdon and Kathleen Whiteside	The LIFE Company	LIFE Restructuring	Insurance	HPI implementation
Curtiss S. Peck	Harley-Davidson	You Can Teach Old Dogs New Tricks—You Just Need Different Methods	Manufacturing	Performance coaching
Marilyn Kerr and Jeremie Hill Grey	Motorola Semiconductor	Developing Strategic Software Skills in Support of SEI	Semiconductor manufacturing	Competency modeling

Stephen B. King	Peabody Processing Incorporated	Improving Roll Changeover Performance in a Manufacturing Organization	Manufacturing	Work redesign
Calvin C. Hoffman and John M. Stormes	Southern California Gas Company	Responding to Competitive Pressures With Integrated HR Systems	Utility	Integrated systems approach to human resources
Joseph P. Yaney	General Hospital of Chicago	Solving Health-Care Performance Problems in a Turbulent Environment	Health care	Organization development
Robert J. Rosania	AmeriGas Partners, LLP	Linking Performance Improvement to Cultural Change	Retail propane marketing	Organization development training
Andrea K. Moore and Deborah L. Stone	National Association of Securities Dealers	Human Performance in Action	Securities	Performance support systems

Follow-Up

Due to space limitations, the editors had to omit some information about the cases. Readers who require additional information on any case may contact the authors directly.

Thoughts on Human Performance Improvement

William J. Rothwell and David D. Dubois

Human performance improvement (HPI) means, quite simply, matching the right solution or solutions to the right problem or problems, or using the right approaches to unleash human performance. Many people feel that the term *training*—and even the term *human resource development*—gives the wrong impression about what contributions people in our field can make to line managers, employees, and other key organizational stakeholders. The introduction briefly defines HPI, summarizes the HPI process model (from Rothwell, 1996a), and describes what the model means. The authors also review, briefly, the roles of people who do HPI work and the many performance improvement interventions that may be applied to solving human performance problems or seizing human performance improvement opportunities.

What is human performance improvement? What are the steps in the HPI process model? What roles do people who perform HPI work enact? What range of human performance improvement strategies are possible, and when are they appropriately applied? This introduction answers these key questions and, in doing so, lays the foundation for this case book.

What Is Human Performance Improvement?[1]

Human performance improvement is a "systematic process of discovering and analyzing important human performance gaps, designing and developing cost-effective and ethically justifiable strategies to close those gaps, implementing the strategies, and evaluating the financial and nonfinancial results" (Rothwell, 1996a, p. 79). In this definition, the term *systematic* means that HPI is approached in an organized, rather than incidental, way. *Process* means a continuous activity carried out for a purpose. HPI is carried out to improve human performance. *Discovering and analyzing* mean identifying and examining present and possible future barriers preventing an organization, process, or individual from achieving desired results or outcomes. *Important* implies that priorities are established when time and effort are devoted to seeking improvement opportunities. *Human performance* refers to the end results or accomplishments desired from purposeful behavior or activity. *Gaps* are differences between actual and ideal results. *Designing and developing cost-effective and ethically justifiable strategies* means finding and formulating optimal or desirable ways of solving human performance problems or seizing human performance improvement opportunities. The word *strategy* implies long-term, evolutionary, and progressive change. It is therefore preferable to the word *solution*, which may imply a quick fix (Rothwell, 1996a). *Cost-effective* implies sensitivity to bottom-line improvements by those performing HPI work; *ethically justifiable* implies sensitivity to ethical and moral viewpoints. *Implementing the strategies* means finding the optimal, or most cost-efficient and cost-effective, way to solve human performance problems and achieve desired results. Sometimes called deployment, this step refers to the installation process for human performance improvement strategy. *Evaluating the results* focuses on accountability. Those involved in HPI work always remain keenly aware of the need to gather persuasive evidence of the economic and noneconomic value of their human performance improvement strategies. For that reason they make an effort to forecast expected results before they undertake training or implement other planned human performance improvement strategies.

What Are the Steps in the HPI Process Model?[2]

A model is a simple depiction of an idea, object, or phenomenon that is otherwise more complex. Many models may describe HPI. ASTD's model appears in figure 1. Each step in the model deserves a brief description.

Step 1: Performance Analysis

During performance analysis, those performing HPI work identify and describe human performance gaps (Rothwell, 1996a). In other words, the people who do performance analysis collect information to answer such questions as these (Rothwell, 1996a):

Figure 1. The human performance improvement process.

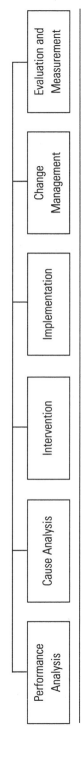

Source: Rothwell, W. (1966). *The ASTD Models for Human Performance Improvement: Roles, Competencies, and Outputs.* Alexandria, VA: The American Society for Training & Development, p. 13.

- Who is affected by the performance gap? Is it one person, a group, an organization, or a work process?
- What is the desired situation? What is the actual situation?
- When and where did the performance first occur—or when and where is it expected to begin? When and where were its effects and side effects (symptoms) and aftereffects (consequences) first noticed? Have they been noticed consistently or inconsistently?
- How has the gap been affecting the organization? Have its effects been widespread or limited? Traceable to individuals, work groups, locations, departments, divisions, suppliers, distributors, customers, or others? What have been the immediate and direct results of the gap?
- How much has the gap been costing the organization? How could the tangible economic impact of the gap be calculated best? How could the intangible impact of the gap be calculated in lost customer goodwill or worker morale?

The outcome of performance analysis should be a clear description of the existing and desired conditions surrounding performance. It should thus answer the following four key questions (Rothwell, 1996a):
—What results (performance outcomes) are actually being achieved?
—What results are desired?
—How large is the performance gap?
—How important is the performance gap?

Step 2: Cause Analysis

The second step in the human performance improvement process model is cause analysis (Rothwell, 1996a). At this point, the people who do cause analysis identify the one or more root causes of a performance gap. In other words, they address such questions as these: why does the performance gap exist? Is the cause a lack of knowledge, skill, or appropriate attitude? a lack of management action? or a combination?

Of course, performance gaps may result from many causes. To determine the causes, those who perform HPI work may consider such issues as these (Rothwell, 1996a):
1. How well do performers see the results or consequences of what they do? Performance gaps can, of course, result when performers do not see how their work helps to meet organizational, work process, or other performers' needs.
2. How well are performers rewarded or provided with incentives for performing as desired? How much do incentives (offered before per-

formance) or rewards (offered after performance) induce performers to achieve desired work results? Are there, in fact, incentives or rewards for achieving the desired results or are performers somehow penalized or otherwise given disincentives for achieving the desired work results?

3. How well are performers given the information or feedback they need to perform at the time they need it? Are performers given important information they need to perform on a timely basis?

4. How well are performers supported in what they do by appropriate environmental resources, equipment, or tools? Do performers have the necessary aids and conditions to perform?

5. How well are individuals or groups able to perform? Do performers have the ability, time, and other resources necessary to perform?

6. How well are performers motivated to perform, and how realistic are their expectations? Do performers want to achieve desired results? What payoffs do they expect from doing that? How realistic are the payoffs they expect?

7. How well do performers' knowledge and skills match up to performance demands? Could performers achieve desired results if their lives depended on it, or do they lack the necessary know-how to perform?

Cause analysis can be carried out using many tools and techniques. One popular approach is to ask performers to trace the causes of a performance gap using a fishbone diagram, like the one in figure 2. Whatever methods people use, the outcome of cause analysis should be a clear description of the causes of the performance gaps.

Step 3: Intervention

The third step in the HPI process model is selecting appropriate interventions (Rothwell, 1996a). (An intervention is a human performance improvement strategy.) In this step, those who perform HPI work consider possible ways to close—or minimize—the performance gap by addressing its root causes. Interventions or human performance improvement strategies may be used individually or in combination, depending on the cause or causes of the gap. Table 1 lists examples of possible root causes of human performance gaps and the corresponding interventions (HPIS) designed to address them.

Step 4: Implementation

The fourth step in the human performance improvement process model is implementation (Rothwell, 1996a). At this point, those per-

Figure 2. The relationship between the human performance improvement process and roles.

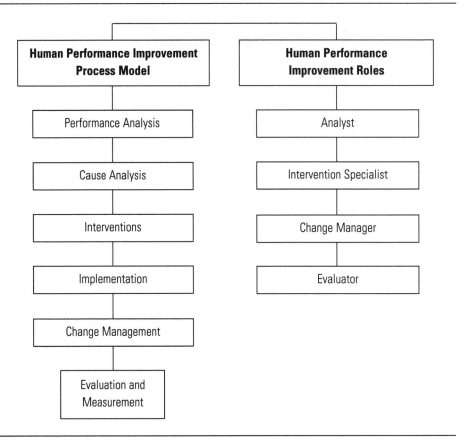

Source: Rothwell, W. (1996). *The ASTD Models for Human Performance Improvement: Roles, Competencies, and Outputs.* Alexandria, VA: The American Society for Training & Development, p. 17.

forming HPI work help the organization prepare to install the intervention or human performance improvement strategy. They may help performers, performers' managers, process owners, and other stakeholders (Rothwell, 1996a) do the following, among other things:

- examine what the organization is presently doing to address the cause of the human performance gap
- determine what the organization should be doing to address the cause of the human performance gap
- assess changes inside or outside the organization that may affect the HPIS as it is implemented

Table 1. Possible causes of human performance gaps and interventions to address them.

Possible Root Cause of a Human Performance Gap	Possible Human Performance Improvement Strategies to Address Root Cause
• Workers are not receiving sufficient information about how well they are performing.	• Improve daily feedback • Examine, and formulate possible improvements in, employee performance appraisal practices. • Examine handling of communication and feedback with one or more of the following: suppliers, customers, distributors, or regulators.
• The organization is experiencing high *critical turnover* (the best workers are leaving) because career paths are unclear.	• Improve career development practices. • Clarify career paths. • Improve succession planning practices.
• Individuals are complaining that they are receiving inconsistent development across work units, teams, departments, divisions, or the organization.	• Improve employee coaching practices.
• The organization's "culture" is commonly faulted by creating complacency, rewarding poor performance, and rewarding behaviors and actions that are not consistent with organizational goals.	• Undertake a long-term effort to "change culture" using the action research model of organization development.
• Individuals or groups complain that they are not rewarded adequately for the results they achieve, the efforts they put in, or the goals the organization desires.	• Examine, and formulate possible improvements in, compensation practices. • Examine, and formulate possible improvements in, the organization's nonfinancial rewards.
• Workers are sabotaging work, defying authority, or otherwise behaving improperly. • Supervisors or team members do not know how to deal with gap behavior.	• Consider, and formulate possible improvements in, worker documentation. • Examine, and formulate possible improvements in, organizational disciplinary practices. • Formulate possible improvements in worker counseling.
• Workers are experiencing increased incidence of work-related health problems or safety problems.	• Formulate possible improvements in environmental engineering factors in the workplace. • Formulate possible improvements in health and safety policies, practices, and training. • Formulate possible improvements in the organization's employee wellness policies and practices.

continued on page 8

Table 1. Possible causes of human performance gaps and interventions to address them (continued).

Possible Root Cause of a Human Performance Gap	Possible Human Performance Improvement Strategies to Address Root Cause
• Workers, customers, suppliers, or distributors are not receiving needed information on a timely basis.	• Formulate possible improvements in the organization's information systems.
• Workers do not possess information or knowledge and skills they need to perform at the time they need to perform.	• Improve the use of job aids. • Formulate possible improvements in training workers. • Formulate possible improvements in the performance-support tools for workers (such as expert systems and context sensitive help).
• Workers complain that they are unable to achieve the results desired because they have too much to do, the tasks are poorly coordinated.	• Formulate possible improvements in the organization's design (who reports to whom). • Formulate possible improvements in the jobs' design (how work tasks are grouped together). • Formulate possible improvements in the way tasks are grouped together (examine work procedures).
• The organization is always "playing catch-up" with competitors. • The organization is rarely "ahead of the curve" with competitors.	• Examine, and formulate possible improvements in, leadership in the organization.
• Workers are entering their jobs without the knowledge and skills they need to learn new work duties. • Workers are being transferred, for short or long timespans, without the knowledge and skills they need to learn new work duties. • Workers are advancing to higher-level positions because of seniority more than because they meet the requirements for advancement. • Workers are leaving the organization because of terminations for poor performance.	• Examine, and formulate possible improvements in, hiring practices. • Examine, and formulate possible improvements in, promotional practices. • Examine, and formulate possible improvements in, succession planning practices. • Examine, and formulate possible improvements in, career development practices. • Examine, and formulate possible improvements in, transfer practices.

continued on page 9

Table 1. Possible causes of human performance gaps and interventions to address them (continued).

Possible Root Cause of a Human Performance Gap	Possible Human Performance Improvement Strategies to Address Root Cause
• Work is not being coordinated effectively within work units or teams or across teams. • Workers do not see how they contribute to meeting organizational or customer needs.	• Examine, and formulate possible improvements in, supervision and management practices. • Examine, and formulate possible improvements in, training for supervisors, managers, and executives. • Examine, and formulate possible improvements in, the organization's planning and communication practices.
• Workers in work units or teams are not interacting effectively. • Executives, managers, or supervisors are in conflict.	• Consider, and formulate possible improvements in, team-building efforts.
• Workers have performed the work previously but, because they must perform a unique task so rarely, they have forgotten what to do.	• Consider, and formulate possible improvements in, having workers practice the task (structured practice). • Consider, and formulate possible improvements in, creating job aids for workers.
• Management has never clarified what work results are expected or desired.	• Consider, and formulate possible improvements in, clarifying job standards and work expectations. • Consider, and formulate possible improvements in, improving the quality and quantity of information given to workers about customers' needs and organizational goals and plans.

- clarify and emphasize how the HPIS will help the organization meet its needs, achieve its mission, and realize strategic planning goals and objectives
- identify best sources of talent and resources to implement the HPIS, such as internal talent, external talent, or some combination.

The outcome of this step is usually a clear sense of the desired outcomes the intervention is to achieve, an action plan that enjoys the ownership of key decision makers and other stakeholders, and the talent necessary to implement the HPIS. The best laid plans for human performance improvement will not come to fruition if this critically important step is mishandled. To be effective, any HPIS requires a long-term commitment and constant oversight by HPI specialists, stakeholders, and decision makers. If they treat HPIS like a quick fix, it will usually fail.

Step 5: Change Management

The fifth step in the human performance improvement process model is change management (Rothwell, 1996a). During this step, those performing HPI work should monitor the intervention or HPI intervention for the following (Rothwell, 1996a):

- How well is the intervention addressing the root causes of human performance gaps? What measurable improvements can be shown?
- How much ownership in HPIS do stakeholders and decision makers enjoy, and what steps can be taken to improve that ownership? What can be done to maintain, or increase, ownership and support for the HPIS?
- How may changing conditions inside and outside the organization affect the success of the HPIS? What is done to improve the HPIS continuously, as it is being implemented, and what is done to keep it centered on desired results amid changing workplace and workforce conditions?

The outcome of this step is usually an HPIS that is managed on a daily basis in a way consistent with desired results.

Step 6: Evaluation and Measurement

The sixth step is evaluation and measurement (Rothwell, 1996a). At this point those performing HPI work take stock of the results HPIS achieved. They consider such questions as these (Rothwell, 1996a):

- How well did the HPIS achieve desired and measurable results?
- How well were the forecasted and measurable improvements targeted for the HPIS realized?
- What side effects of the HPIS were noticed? What were the positive and negative side effects?
- What lessons were learned from the HPIS that could be applied in the future?
- How well has the HPIS been adopted in the corporate culture?
- What best practices or lessons learned resulted from the HPIS?

Evaluation is properly targeted at the subject for change (such as employee performance) and at the HPIS (the means to an end).

It thus answers two key questions: Did results match intentions? and Was the human performance gap closed or narrowed, and were organizational needs met? Measurement determines how much change and how much improvement occurred. What were the impacts of the intervention and HPI strategy? What value was added in economic and noneconomic terms?

The Roles Enacted by Those Who Perform HPI Work[3]

A role is a part played. People play many parts in their lives, such as spouse, child, and parent. Individuals who carry out the HPI process enact four key roles (Rothwell, 1996a):

- analyst
- intervention specialist
- change manager
- evaluator.

They are related to steps in the HPI process model, as figure 2 shows. Each part deserves a brief explanation.

The Role of Analyst

This role conducts troubleshooting to isolate one or more causes of human performance gaps or identify areas in which human performance can be improved (Rothwell, 1996a, p. 17). It encompasses both performance analysis and cause analysis.

The Role of Intervention Specialist

This role "selects appropriate interventions to address the root cause(s) of performance gaps" (Rothwell, 1996a, p. 17). It is linked to the intervention step in the HPI process model.

The Role of Change Manager

This role "ensures that interventions are implemented in ways consistent with desired results and that they help individuals and groups achieve results" (Rothwell, 1996a, p. 17). It is linked to the intervention and implementation steps in the HPI process model.

The Role of Evaluator

This role "assesses the impact of interventions and follows up on changes made, actions taken, and results achieved in order to provide participants and stakeholders with information about how well interventions are being implemented" (Rothwell, 1996a, p. 17).

The Range of Human Performance Improvement Strategies

A human performance improvement strategy is a solution to a human performance problem or a means by which to realize a human performance improvement opportunity. A human performance improvement strategy is appropriately identified through cause analysis. But what causes of human performance problems provide clues about what performance improvement interventions to use?

Possible Causes of Human Performance Problems

Examine the left column in table 1. Note that there are many possible causes of human performance problems. It is only possible to "fix" a performance problem by addressing its cause—not by addressing its "symptoms." (High turnover, for example, is a symptom, not a problem. It is only possible to reduce turnover by discovering and addressing the cause.) It is worth emphasizing at this point that one cause of human performance problems is lack of knowledge, skill, or appropriate attitude.

Possible Performance Improvement Strategies

Examine the right column in the table. Note that causes stem from deficiencies in the world inside or the world outside the performer. Training is an appropriate performance improvement strategy only when the cause of the problem stems from lack of knowledge, skill, or ability. More often than not, performance improvement strategies require management action. This action is necessary because management controls the environment surrounding workers and thereby affects the conditions under which individuals perform. For that reason, many observers of the HPI field draw attention to the need to establish a high-performance workplace—that is, a work environment in which individuals are able to (and indeed encouraged to) perform to their peak.

Summary

The introduction has addressed the following questions:

- What is human performance improvement?
- What are the steps in the HPI process model?
- What roles are enacted by those who perform HPI work?
- What range of human performance improvement strategies are possible, and when are they appropriately applied?

The definition of HPI is a systematic process of discovering and analyzing important human performance gaps, designing and developing cost-effective and ethically justifiable strategies to close those gaps, implementing the strategies and evaluating the financial and nonfinancial results (Rothwell, 1996a, p. 79). There are six steps in the HPI process model: performance analysis; cause analysis; intervention; implementation; change management; and evaluation and measurement. The HPI roles correspond approximately to the steps in the HPI process model. Accordingly, individuals who perform HPI work may enact such roles as analyst, intervention specialist, change manager, and evaluator.

A human performance improvement strategy is a solution to a human performance problem or is a means by which to realize a human performance improvement opportunity. A human performance improvement strategy is appropriately identified through cause analysis.

Notes
[1]This section is adapted from Rothwell, 1996a.
[2]This section is adapted from Rothwell, 1996a.
[3]This section is adapted from Rothwell, 1996a.

References
Consulted for the Introduction
Dubois, D.D. (1993). *Competency-Based Performance Improvement.* Amherst, MA: Human Resource Development Press.

Dubois, D.D., editor. (1998). *The Competency Case Book: Twelve Studies in Competency-Based Performance Improvement.* Amherst, MA: Human Resource Development Press.

Robinson, D., and J. Robinson. (1995). *Performance Consulting: Moving Beyond Training.* San Francisco: Berrett-Koehler.

Rothwell, W. (1996a). *The ASTD Models for Human Performance Improvement: Roles, Competencies, and Outputs.* Alexandria, VA: The American Society for Training & Development.

Rothwell, W. (1996b). *Beyond Training and Development: State-of-the-Art Strategies for Enhancing Human Performance.* New York: AMACOM.

Additional Resources on Human Performance Improvement
Callahan, M. (1997). "From Training to Performance Consulting," INFO-LINE. No. 9702. Alexandria, VA: American Society for Training & Development.

Callahan, M. (1997). "The Role of the Performance Intervention Specialist," INFO-LINE. No. 9714. Alexandria, VA: American Society for Training & Development.

Kirrane, D. (1997). "The Role of the Performance Needs Analyst," INFO-LINE. No. 9713. Alexandria, VA: American Society for Training & Development.

Koehle, D. (1997). "The Role of the Performance Change Manager," INFO-LINE. No. 9715. Alexandria, VA: American Society for Training & Development.

Langdon, D. (1997). "A Look Into the Future of Human Performance Technology." *Performance Improvement, 36*(6), 6-9.

Risher, H., and C. Fay. (1995). *The Performance Imperative: Strategies for Enhancing Workforce Effectiveness.* San Francisco: Jossey-Bass.

Robinson, D., and J. Robinson. (1995). *Performance Consulting: Moving Beyond Training.* San Francisco: Berrett-Koehler.

Spitzer, D. (1996). "Ensuring Successful Performance Improvement Interventions." *Performance Improvement, 35*(9), 26-27.

Westgaard, O. (1997). "Describing a Performance Improvement Specialist: The Heurist." *Performance Improvement, 36*(6), 10-15.

Woods, J., and J. Cortada, editors. (1997). *The ASTD Training and Performance Yearbook 1997.* New York: McGraw-Hill.

Implementation of Workplace Education in a Small Manufacturing Company

Danby Tool

Dale C. Brandenburg

The implementation of workplace education programs is very seldom a straightforward process. There are always unexpected conditions that may enhance or inhibit the process of implementation. There were three reasons for documenting the implementation process here. First, this site was part of the launch of an extended program transcending other small company sites. Second, such documentation would assist in making sure that human resource leaders of the target company and future team members of the implementing organization had the advantage of lessons learned. The third reason was to attempt to generalize the findings to situations where workplace education is needed.

Background

Workplace education is the generally accepted term for what was once known as workplace literacy, other types of literacy, or pretechnical instruction conducted in the workplace. This type of instruction is differentiated from adult basic education, which is purely academic in nature; instead, workplace education uses the context of a job to teach the needed fundamental skills.

The subject of this case is implementation, not the design of the instruction or the analysis of skills used to build the curriculum. The focus is on implementation strategy or process steps to be tested and evaluated. A small manufacturing plant was used for a number of reasons, including that there are more than 300 times as many plants

This case was prepared to serve as a basis for discussion rather than to illustrate either effective or ineffective administrative and management practices. The organization and some names have been disguised at the request of the author.

of this type (especially those with fewer than 500 employees) than there are plants with 1,000 or more employees. Second, such facilities have a difficult time sustaining an effort once a pilot program has demonstrated success. Understanding the elements of implementation, the support system needed, and identification of key personnel would provide some framework for sustaining the process at this plant and possibly others. A third reason is that human resource development as a field needs to understand the issues facing smaller companies because they are the most likely source of increasing employment opportunities for the foreseeable future.

Another important reason for understanding and generalizing from the implementation issue is that workplace education programs have shown questionable returns-on-investment for the implementing organization (Hollenbeck, 1993), although consistent positive returns exist for the individual participant and for society (Hollenbeck, 1993; Mikulecky & Lloyd, 1993). Thus, an organization, more specifically, its decision makers with resource allocation responsibility, must be convinced of the payoff. The best way to ensure this payoff is to tie workplace education to the business needs. This link is usually possible with the typical training project, but because workplace education is not job specific, it isn't possible to measure its immediate impact in the same terms with the same timeline as job-specific training.

Thus, the costs of implementation for workplace education in small companies, which typically have resource constraints, must be minimal, and the formal process must be simple. Introducing complexity to the point of comprehensiveness is likely to be self-defeating for the small company and for the service provider.

Organizational Profile

Danby Tool is the Detroit-based subsidiary of a larger, family-owned company. Because it is the only plant located in Michigan, its isolation and the fact that it is the only automotive supplier of the Danby Group and the only unionized facility mean that it operates quite independently. The only overlapping administration is at the board of directors level. Approximately 195 of its 230 employees are members of a United Auto Workers (UAW) local that represents a considerable number of other small automotive suppliers. Revenues for 1996 were approximately $24 million.

Danby belongs to the industry category known as metal forming or stamping, and its main line of products is gears for truck transmissions. The company produces no final parts, but occasionally some subassemblies. The major machines stamp parts on middle-sized presses rated at less than 100 tons. Other machines include some computer numerically controlled mills that perform some grinding operations. Most of its machines have computerized controllers, that is, single function computers that are electronically programmed. The company designs and builds the dies that it uses in the presses. Its ability to design and build parts to unique specifications requires that the general skill level of the plant be high; most employees have high school degrees or higher. Stamping presses are very noisy, creating a monotonous "ka-chung, ka-chung" that can be heard and felt throughout the entire facility. All employees and visitors to the shop floor must wear safety glasses and earplugs.

Danby participates in typical industry associations like the Precision Metalforming Association (primarily for small metal-stamping firms) and also belongs to a unique regional association of other small unionized manufacturing firms called the Labor-Management Council for Economic Renewal (LMCER). This membership organization is sponsored by the UAW Region 1A (the region covers most of Wayne, Monroe, Lenawee, and Washtenaw counties in extreme southeastern Michigan). Its purpose is to promote best practices of labor-management cooperation through a wide range of learning opportunities and shared information. Danby is considered a leader among the LMCER companies in attempting best human resource practices, although it does not have a strategic training plan or any specific programs that address literacy, basic skills, or pretechnical education.

It is unusual for a company of Danby's size to have 2.5 full-time equivalent staff devoted to human resource functions. Although Danby is considered a leader among its local peer group of companies, from outside the company both union and nonunion personnel have criticized it for not following through on a number of innovative practices. The former union plant chair described Danby as typical of many other small auto suppliers that "get jerked around by their major customer and institute the 'flavor of the month program' to keep the customer off their backs." It is not unusual for small auto suppliers to start one improvement program only to back off because of short-term financial woes, delivery pressures, or increased quality standards. Danby seemed more prone to the whims of its management than other companies in its industry. On a more positive note, most employees tended to be long term, and there have been very few layoffs over the past 10 years or so. Labor-management relations at the plant are positive, and there has not been any significant labor unrest in the past 10 years. The typical unionized employee has 14 or more years of service. There is a tuition assistance program for management employees, but none for the unionized employees. Once a year or so the company offered or mandated training to represented employees, often on released time and never at the company site.

From a cultural perspective, Danby is one of those companies where the quality and consistency of union leadership have generally exceeded those of management leadership. Top management leaders typically last less than four years, and there is frequent turnover at other levels, especially shop-floor supervisors. Every few months, a union leader is asked if he wants a promotion to supervisor, and he usually refuses. One exception to this management turnover is the manager of human resources, and this may in turn account for the positive relationship between union and management.

Trigger Events

Although Danby experiences minimal turnover of represented employees, the company always needs more skilled tradespeople—the die makers and maintenance personnel who are experienced with advanced tools and electronic devices. Their skill level in many respects is comparable to that of a manufacturing engineer with knowledge of blueprint interpretation, programmable cutting tools, sophisticated measuring devices, process capability analysis, and process documentation procedures. Such employees earn about $8 per hour more than a typical production hourly employee does. Danby has found it difficult to recruit such skilled workers from outside the company because of its location in Detroit, financial instability, and somewhat lower wages than those paid to skill tradespeople who work at the Big Three. The company's preference was to recruit the needed apprentices from those already in the company because it could ensure their commitment as an apprentice and pay them lower wages than demanded externally.

About every 18 months, Steve Mint, the director of human resources, would cooperatively sponsor with the union committee a testing session to determine if at least four to five of the current employees could qualify for the internal apprentice program. To sign up for the test, an employee had to have at least two years of seniority. The testing process to qualify as an apprentice was a contractual issue, and, therefore, a nonnegotiable component. Generally, 20 to 25 employees signed up for these testing sessions. An optional class of approximately 10 hours of basic math skills was made available to employees to take on their own time prior to the testing session. The standard for passing this exam and qualifying for an apprenticeship position was by agreement with the union plant committee, led by Mike Williams (the shop committee chair) and Mint.

The testing session held in the summer of 1994 did not go well. Only two employees passed the test with sufficiently high scores for selection to the five open apprenticeship slots. Williams requested an analysis of all the scores to determine what caused this result. An outside vendor performed a detailed examination, which showed that almost two-thirds of the employees failed to get 50 percent of the math section correct, and more than one-third obtained low scores on a verbal section. Although both Williams and Mint suspected this problem, especially with math, they now had evidence to go to senior management with a request for something to help solve it.

A month or so later, Williams and Mint attended a special session on regional training resources sponsored by LMCER. There they heard of the workplace education program run by Wayne State University (WSU). Following meetings and negotiations, Danby entered into a contract with WSU to help improve the results of succeeding apprentice qualification sessions.

Setting the Stage

The WSU team was interested both in helping Danby solve its apprenticeship qualification issue and in leaving in place a system that could be sustained and reconstituted for this need or others of the same type. This meant that the front-end analysis had to be more than an examination of instructional skill needs and a performance task analysis. Although those steps were necessary to create a high-quality instructional package, they would not address systemic organizational context issues likely to be present. Thus, the front-end process was to be more of a performance analysis than just a standard needs assessment.

WSU saw one major objective of the effort to "teach" the major human resource functionaries in the organization how to plan, implement, and customize the approach to meet a specific need. The major players in the process at Danby were Mint, Williams (and some of his union shop committee members), and what turned out to be the "nebulous" senior management at this Danby site. Three other people who had major roles at different stages were part of the WSU team: Irene Sinclair, the assistant director for instruction (the chief contact and implementer), Nancy Ruetz, the assistant director for curriculum (developer of instruction and leader of the needs assessment team), and Chauncey Cooper (the instructor). Sinclair and Ruetz were experienced educators, who together had 50 years of adult education experience. Ruetz had just completed five years of designing and leading a workplace literacy program at a large manufacturing facility. Sinclair was new to manufacturing plant sites, greasy floors, sexist language, and the use of safety glasses and earplugs. She began getting acclimated to the Danby environment by collecting the needs assessment data from a number of plants and helping to set up a few pilot classes at other sites. Besides, Sinclair was brimming with enthusiasm and energy, always using her outgoing personality to cover for her lack of shop-floor experience; production hourly employees accepted her quickly and willingly.

Analyzing the Performance Problem

Williams, Mint, Sinclair, and Ruetz planned the initial data-collection process. The instruments used consisted of interviews with key production and skilled trades employees (a total of 11 were interviewed), interviews with all shop-floor supervisors (there were seven covering the two shifts), an observation schedule (a detailed walk-through of the plant), and individual interviews with Mint and Williams. The employee interview had 112 questions and lasted from 20 minutes to an hour; the interview schedule for the supervisors, Williams and Mint, was about two-thirds that length.

The results of Sinclair and Ruetz's needs assessment did not surprise any of the key players. Low scores on the apprentice qualification test were one manifestation of a larger problem. Almost two-thirds of the interviewees reported that an attempt to implement statistical process control (SPC) 18 months earlier using a 40-hour released time training course met with dismal failure. The SPC implementation called for substantial involvement from everyone on the shop floor. When the SPC data were not being recorded correctly, Mint and Williams worked out a sample performance situation to gauge the level of understanding as practiced on the job. They found that fewer than 25 percent of shop-floor personnel could correctly enter or interpret the SPC data for their own workstations. The general level of mathematics understanding was considerably below what was needed to perform many key tasks. Although reading skills were determined to be less than tenth-grade proficiency, they were adequate for most current job tasks.

These findings led Mint to recommend to senior management that Danby must defer the implementation of SPC to the shop floor, although it was continued in the front office. There were significant business implications for this decision. It meant that Danby would not be ready to begin for at least another year the process of qualifying for the QS 9000 quality standards recently announced by the Big Three automakers. These standards are much more rigorous than previous ones because auditors actually question shop-floor personnel at random. Not having all shop-floor employees familiar with company statistical procedures would run the risk of failure to qualify. Postponing the qualification process would risk future company business if the timeline for small auto-supplier certification was not met. Union leaders were not pleased with Mint's decision to leave this problem unresolved because they knew that all Danby personnel would have to go through similar training and implementation in the future. Thus, it provided another example of failure of management follow-through.

The most consistent finding from the data collection was a lack of an organizational infrastructure, commitment, and past history for implementing and retaining needed solutions to problems (Brandenburg & Binder, 1992). This gap was just as likely with regard to new machines, safety, or tools as it was to human performance issues. Even though the issue of QS 9000 was certainly business related, there always seemed to be a reason for changing or dropping a program before it could produce results. It was common practice at Danby to start a project and obtain union buy-in and support, resources from management, and quality training, and then to drop the effort without full implementation or observation of its effectiveness.

Mint and Williams were committed to moving forward with the apprenticeship preparation class even though it answered an immediate need for a smaller business problem. They, with Ruetz and Sinclair, reasoned that 60 percent or so of this class would focus on job-related basic mathematics, the same kind of math needed to fulfill the missing background component for implementing SPC in the future. Starting with apprenticeship preparation would not be wasted time. Some materials could be used in developing the SPC program, and company culture and contextual issues would have already been built in. Ruetz and Sinclair saw the strong need to have one program at Danby recognized as an implementation success. The opportunity to create such a process provided additional incentive for Ruetz and Sinclair to create the solution Williams and Mint wanted.

Determining the instructional components, performing the task analysis, developing and testing the materials, and hiring and coaching the right instructor were relatively straightforward tasks for Ruetz and Sinclair. Keeping the apprentice preparation program going on a yearly basis or whenever it was needed proved to be more difficult than expected.

Components of Implementation

Sinclair and Ruetz, with the help of some their colleagues at the university, created a general picture of implementation. This picture of implementation system components, shown as figure 1, was based on experience in other workplace education and industrial relations programs. The figure shows seven components for the implementation process: staff development, instructional delivery, recruitment, incentives, resources, organizational constraints, and union and management relations. Instructional delivery and staff development are the two obvious components. The remaining factors sometimes receive less attention, but as will be seen in the Danby situation, hold equal or greater importance. A brief description of each component is given below.

Figure 1. Implementation system components.

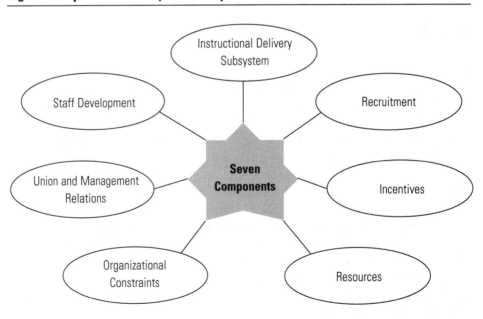

Instructional Delivery

Instructional delivery consists of the curriculum and methods used to deliver the instruction, such as instructor's manuals, participant guides, and computer courseware. The design of the curriculum materials at Danby followed a modified whole language approach.

The whole language philosophy provides a unique approach for developing the learner. It supports success in the classroom, on the job, and at home. The instructor is regarded as a facilitator of learning rather than the major source of knowledge and information. Recognizing and building upon participants' unique past experiences are crucial for integrating new learning. In this process, continual dialogue and interaction are key to the instructional process. The curriculum is built on the learners' strengths, not weaknesses, and accommodates the variety of learning styles and cultural orientations. It also encourages each learner to assume responsibility for his or her own learning. Recognition of success in the classroom enables learners to feel good about themselves. Learners become empowered workers by understanding the job process and how they contribute to the big picture.

Staff Development

This is the process of establishing standards or criteria for instructors, the selection, hiring and training of these instructors, and then some continuing staff development activities (Powers, 1992; Yelon, 1996). Chauncey Cooper, the Danby instructor, had recently retired from the public-sector's Job Training Partnership Act (JTPA) program and had been teaching adults for more than 25 years. He was perfect for the job because as a quiet, but knowledgeable teacher, he was nonthreatening, adaptable to a wide variety of situations, and unassuming. He came across to the workers as a father figure, mentor, and advisor, thus making his role as a facilitator an easy one to perform. He needed to be coached in using the whole language approach, but found it to fit his style quite well.

Recruitment

The purpose of the recruitment process is to notify employees of upcoming educational opportunities and to enroll them in the program. Its long-term goal is to get instruction like this to be part of the regular instructional plan, not an adjunct to it. Internal plant employees (called advocates or liaisons) performed most efficiently in recruiting people for the courses and in identifying potential implementation problems. This means that the process of recruitment begins long before the first course is ready to be delivered. Other elements of recruitment could include use of the company newsletter or mailings to employees, holding open houses to show what is available, having an in-house project advocate who is going to be the point person available for other employees to answer questions, using a general plantwide announcement meeting, or personal interaction with employees on the shop floor.

At the outset of the Danby recruitment process, Sinclair and Ruetz identified Jack Burns, a needs assessment interviewee, as a good candidate for the advocate position. Burns had failed the apprentice qualification test twice, but was determined to pass the next time. He was vocal and assertive in positive ways, and his co-workers liked him. His 15 years of seniority also meant that he knew the plant personnel and culture very well. He provided advice and counsel to Sinclair, and, as he said, he could "teach her a few things about manufacturing shop floor politics."

Incentives

The company or union, or both, need to demonstrate their commitment to the class by offering incentives of some sort to employees who participate. This kind of commitment needs to be obtained up-front so there is some tangible benefit to employees who participate. Incentives can be varied to include release time, opportunities for job advancement, cash incentives, recognition, personal motivation for self-improvement, and tuition assistance programs.

At Danby, Mint, Williams, and Sinclair developed a plan for two hours of instruction twice a week. One hour was on released time, and the second hour was not. The added incentive was the potential for being selected to the apprenticeship program through passing their exam.

Resources

Resources are the physical and fiscal support mechanisms, which include the funding for the program, facilities or space, computer labs, a bulletin board to post announcements, and secondary support available in the form of career counseling, materials, or resources provided by vendors to the organization.

At Danby, the union plant committee organized a group of volunteers to remake a storage room into a classroom. The committee added a white board, some electrical outlets, and an old file cabinet.

It modified the ductwork to obtain sufficient heat and cleaned the walls and floor. Because the classroom was located in the shop-floor area, up one level, there was little to be done to shut out the noise. Sinclair and Cooper were initially concerned about the monotonous "ka-chung," but they soon got just as immune to it as the workers attending the classes.

Organizational Constraints

Organizational constraints include both planned and unplanned events that occur during the implementation process. Value to program delivery is increased through understanding the organizational culture and then delivering a program consistent with that culture. There are many issues beyond the implementer's control that can be anticipated and prepared for so that adjustments can be made and the credibility of the program maintained. These include changes in business priorities, swing shifts, summer work schedules, strikes, changes in key personnel, short-term company financial problems, and plantwide shutdowns.

Two events of this type occurred at Danby. Nine months into instructional delivery, Sinclair was informed that the classes were to be suspended for an undetermined time because there was a short-term cash-flow problem. Three months later when instruction resumed, Earl Smith was elected to the union plant chair position, replacing Williams. Smith was not nearly as committed to the program as Williams, and was less likely to make strong demands on management for its continuance.

Union and Management Relations

Working with joint union-management committees can be extremely beneficial in establishing a program that meets the needs of both union and management. Committee meetings can be a valuable and important forum in which to present ideas on how to schedule instructional delivery and permit cooperation to resolve issues such as seniority, downtime, recruitment, identification and training of advocates, and approval of data-collection instruments. Another important activity is developing a method for the reinforcement of learning with front-line supervisors. Objectives are to assure employees that their attendance is recognized and that a supportive feedback loop is in place to encourage further learning.

Two meetings, a supervisor orientation and a supervisor follow-up, were used to make sure front-line supervisors understood what employees would learn in the classes and how they could support the new learning behavior. The follow-up session was scheduled to get feedback and suggestions from the supervisors to improve the ongoing program.

Timeline for Key Events

Table 1 shows key dates for the implementation process at Danby. Danby probably needed to run the apprentice preparation class on at least a yearly basis to ensure sufficient numbers for the apprentice program. The union was very supportive of the program throughout and made sure that recruiting was performed fairly, incentives were provided, and the testing process was handled in an equitable manner. However, Mint and other management personnel had responsibility to initiate the program and provide the supporting infrastructure. Mint, Williams, and later Smith thought that the implementation process set up by the WSU team matched their needs quite well and that a sound customer-vendor relationship had been established.

Table 1. Key dates for implementation.

Summer 1994	Apprentice test results show only two employees qualified.
Fall 1994	Mint and Williams attend LMCER training resource session.
Late fall 1994	Ruetz is contacted to negotiate Danby program.
Winter 1995	Ruetz and Sinclair collect needs assessment data.
Late winter 1995	Apprentice class developed; plans finalized; classroom built.
Spring 1995	Recruiting by Burns, Sinclair, and Williams; first classes delivered.
Spring 1995	Regular apprentice test; 6 out of 40 pass—all class participants.
Summer 1995	Classes suspended due to vacation schedules.
Fall 1995	Second group of classes initiated.
Late fall 1995	Mint suspended classes for five months.
Late winter 1996	Classes resume; refresher and tutorials added; Smith elected.
Spring 1996	Regular apprentice test; 4 out of 20 pass—all class participants.
Summer 1996	Danby initiates SPC course for team leaders and key employees.
Fall 1996	Danby cancels class four months to work on QS 9000 certification.
Winter 1997	Danby initiates interpersonal communications class for teams.
Fall 1997	Danby receives QS 9000 certification.
Winter 1998	New apprentice class initiated; test scheduled for spring 1998.

For 18 months, starting in the spring of 1995, the process was slow, with many starts and stops. But from late spring 1996 on, activity accelerated. To prepare for Danby's QS 9000 certification audit, new classes in SPC, which Cooper taught, were started for the shop-floor personnel. Because many of them had attended the apprenticeship class, the number of individuals needing refresher training in the mathematics for SPC was greatly reduced. The classes were completed by early winter 1997. Additionally, Danby desired to renew its team structure, so Mint called on Sinclair once again to deliver an interpersonal communication and problem solving (IPC) class for every employee in the plant. IPC was an existing class in the WSU program used at two other sites. The IPC classes were suspended when Danby received its QS 9000 certification in fall 1997 after 40 percent of the plant had attended classes.

Results

Mint, Williams, and Smith viewed the results of the initial delivery of the apprentice preparation class very positively. Six months after the first set of results, Sinclair interviewed 12 former class participants, including the four selected for the apprentice program. She found some dramatic impacts in a number of cases. Three of the four apprentices were still on the job and also enrolled in community colleges pursuing associate's degrees. The apprentice who left the company moved to Ohio and was apprenticing in another manufacturing plant there. Burns, the advocate and recruiter, passed the test, but had to withdraw from consideration due to an illness in the family. Three months later, he enrolled in a preapprentice program at a local community college. Midlevel management acknowledged his role in the program when they asked him to take over a vacant supervisor position. Burns declined and told Sinclair, "I know I'm a little crazy, but not that crazy." Others Sinclair interviewed expressed very positive feelings toward the program, and of the eight not selected to participate in the apprentice program, three had enrolled in academic adult education classes. Additionally, more than half expressed some positive transfer to their home life. They talked about helping their kids with homework more and with learning to use a home computer.

In the spring of 1995, after the first test results were completed, Sinclair asked one of the Danby brothers what he thought of the findings and learned that he had not heard of the classes. That is, more than one year after the program had started, a room in his plant had been refurbished, and 20 percent of the employees were participating in the first-ever training for hourly employees conducted on-site, he didn't know anything about it. When she asked Mint why the owner didn't know what was going on, Mint said that he didn't think it was important enough to carry it to that level.

However, when senior management pressured Mint to get the plant floor ready for QS 9000 certification, he quickly reinstituted the implementation system that Sinclair and Ruetz had modeled for the apprenticeship class. Mint and Smith were able to put together a program that met business needs because certification was completed within one year after its initiation. They also started the IPC program in the same way. Nonetheless, when certification was received, the only class maintained through the present was the apprenticeship preparation.

Summary

The general objective of the project was to demonstrate to appropriate Danby personnel a process for setting up and maintaining an educational program that was linked to company objectives. The program would be mutually beneficial to the union and to management and be matched to the company culture. Participants (target audience) would be involved in all phases and develop ownership for its continuation. A process was set up that could be generalized to other small companies. Results of the first two rounds of apprenticeship preparation instruction showed that the program could meet the objectives outlined. The most difficult phase was to link the program to a strategic training plan, or at least model how that could be accomplished. This objective was not met until the pressure to attain QS 9000 certification was initiated. With the institution of the SPC and IPC classes, Mint, with Smith's help, found that the implementation model met both company and union needs.

Lessons Learned

Following the first three years of cooperation with Danby, the WSU team conducted a debriefing session to match the implementation model against the results achieved at Danby. Sinclair, Ruetz, Cooper, and their colleagues at the university came up with the following list:
- There is no one sequential set of steps to implementation; each site is likely to have its own peculiarities.
- More than one component will need attention simultaneously, so actions have to be prioritized.

- Recruitment and retention, through incentives, will take as much effort as the instructional development and much more time than delivery.
- Recruitment must begin at least two months before day 1 of class 1.
- Labor-management relations and cooperative problem resolution begin with the process of needs assessment.
- The process of linking needs assessment to program requirements is ongoing and has many implications in the formation of the implementation plan.
- Needs must be linked to business requirements; this is the key method for workplace education to have an integral role in the business.
- The delineation of goals and objectives of the program is better postponed until relationships have been set up with the various stakeholders in the organization; thus, concentrate on meeting only the initial "triggering" need.

Questions for Discussion

1. Compare figure 1 to the six-point model in Gilbert's book (1978). Which factors are matched and which are not? Can you offer an explanation for any missing components?
2. How does the on-again, off-again program implementation at Danby contrast with its reputation as a leader in human resources strategies in the region? Can this pattern be expected just because Danby is a small company?
3. How would you characterize Mint's relationship with top-level management? What could be changed about this relationship to develop a more consistent training strategy?
4. How would you characterize the role of the union leadership in the overall process? Do you see some improvements in the program to benefit both union members and the company?

The Author

Dale C. Brandenburg is research professor of instructional technology at Wayne State University in Detroit. He directs a program in workplace education serving small- and medium-sized manufacturers in the inner city. He specializes in needs assessment, technical training strategy, brokering for small company networks, and the impact of technology deployment. He has completed more than 100 publications and presentations in human performance and training, especially training evaluation. He received his B.S. degree (1966) in mathematics and his M.A. degree (1968) in behavioral psychology, both from Michigan State University, and his Ph.D. degree (1972) in educational measurement and statistics from the University of Iowa. For the past eight years, Brandenburg has devoted his energy to improving the competitiveness of small manufacturing firms through work with the National Center for Manufacturing Sciences, the Michigan Manufacturing Technology Center, the U.S. Air Force, U.S. Department of Commerce, the United Auto Workers Labor-Management Council, and now with Wayne State University. He currently manages training assistance programs for small manufacturers in Detroit. He is a long-term member of the International Society for Performance Improvement. He can be contacted at the following address: Wayne State University, 5425 Gallen Mall, Detroit, MI 58202.

References

Brandenburg, D.C., and C. Binder. (1992). "Emerging Trends in Human Performance Interventions." In Harold D. Stolovitch and Erica J. Keeps (editors), *Handbook of Human Performance Technology* (pp. 651-671). San Francisco: Jossey-Bass.

Gilbert, T.F. (1978). *Human Competence: Engineering Worthy Performance*. New York: McGraw-Hill.

Hollenbeck, K. (1993). *Classrooms in the Workplace*. Kalamazoo, MI: W.E. Upjohn Institute for Employment Research.

Mikulecky, L., and P. Lloyd. (1993). *The Impact of Workplace Literacy Programs: A New Model for Evaluating the Impact of Workplace Literacy Programs*. Philadelphia: National Center on Adult Literacy, University of Pennsylvania.

Powers, B. (1992). *Instructor Excellence*. San Francisco: Jossey-Bass.

Yelon, S.L. (1996). *Powerful Principles of Instruction*. White Plains, NY: Longman.

Developing a Leadership Curriculum

Three-Five Systems, Inc.

Jeremie Hill Grey, Elizabeth A. Sharp, Jennifer Fox Kennedy

This case describes a leadership integration and development project in a fast-paced and progressive high-technology company. The project was designed to support its rapid growth and strategic objectives, and to institutionalize desired values and culture. A task team of committed managers supported by a facilitator and instructional designers defined the characteristics of the ideal leader, operationalized values and cultural attributes, and supervised the development of a leadership curriculum and learning tools for the company. The performance support intervention included compensation and recruiting tools designed to mold and reward desired behaviors and assist in selection and hiring of appropriate candidates. The training developed for the company supported rapid integration of new managers into the Three-Five culture.

Background

Headquartered in Tempe, Arizona, Three-Five Systems, Inc., designs and manufactures user interface devices for operational control and information display functions in products of original equipment manufacturers (OEMs). The company specializes in liquid crystal display (LCD) and light-emitting diode (LED) components and technology, providing its custom design and manufacturing services for customers in the communications, medical electronics, industrial process control, wireless data collection, and office automation marketplaces. Its components are used in products such

This case was prepared to serve as a basis for discussion rather than to illustrate either effective or ineffective administrative and management practices.

as cellular phones, pagers, medical equipment, TVs, VCRs, automotive equipment, and industrial and military controls. About 90 percent of the company's business involves creating custom devices for OEMs in the United States and Europe, but Three-Five also makes some standard devices, including solid-state lamps (used for indicator or status lights), bar graph displays, numeric displays, and infrared emitters used for such devices as smoke detectors and industrial equipment safety devices. Its broadening customer base includes numerous major American and European corporations.

The company's principal assembly facilities are located in Manila, the Philippines, where it operates a state-of-the-art, low-cost manufacturing operation that employs manufacturing techniques such as chip on board, surface mount, through hole, flip chip, and chip on glass. Custom LCD glass is shipped to this facility where it is typically integrated with driver electronics into a product with other devices such as touch panels, keypads, plastic housings, and front panels.

At its corporate headquarters in Tempe, Arizona, the company operates the largest LCD-glass manufacturing line in North America. In addition to providing custom LCD glass for use by Three-Five in the manufacture of display modules in Manila, the Tempe facility allows new designs and technologies from the company's research and development group (also in Tempe) to be immediately transferred to a functioning LCD manufacturing line.

Three-Five's design, development, manufacturing, and assembly expertise has evolved over the past 12 years. The company began in 1986 as III-V Semiconductor, Inc., when a group of investors purchased the optoelectronic division of National Semiconductor. The company's name referred to the elements gallium and arsenide, which are located in the periodic table's group III and V, respectively. These elements were the basic materials in the company's original products. In the late 1980s, new management was brought in, the company was restructured and renamed, and it began to focus on the development of its custom display capabilities. In 1990, the company became publicly traded. From 1990 to 1995, the company grew from $17 million in sales revenue to $91 million. In 1997, Three-Five Systems was named as one of America's fastest-growing companies (Hoover's Business Press, 1997).

The rate of growth created a number of challenges for Three-Five Systems. Among them was the need to develop a leadership culture of its own and a means to rapidly integrate the number of managers recruited from other corporations. Although the leadership team demonstrated considerable strength, most leaders were recruited for their technical and business expertise rather than for their leadership traits, and they came from a variety of companies that had sharply disparate management philosophies. Three-Five sought a method for defining its own distinctive leadership characteristics and institutionalizing them through application of its training and reward systems. Development of a leadership curriculum assumed great importance given the expected 25 percent growth of the company.

Three-Five Objectives

The company's stated objectives for this project were to provide a series of strategic training and development tools to help leaders to:
- understand and accept the company position on employee policies and practices
- successfully explain and support company policies and procedures to employees
- improve leadership skills and effectiveness, particularly in the areas of stress reduction and change management
- understand the requirements, knowledge, and skills for recruitment and selection of key new hires for Three-Five Systems.

Population and Intervention Design

Given the company's objectives, the first steps for the consultants, authors Grey and Kennedy, were to analyze the population and on the basis of data, design an appropriate intervention that would define desired behaviors, establish appropriate performance management systems, and make necessary training and development activities available.

Population

Three-Five Systems, as a young company, had several hundred employees domestically, and another hundred internationally. The domestic Three-Five leadership team consisted of approximately six executives, 12 directors, and 24 managers, with a few supervisors. Another half dozen managers and supervisors were resident in the Philippines. Most members of the leadership team had university degrees in technical fields, with some previous leadership training and experience, most gained in other technical companies with varying leadership philosophies and training systems.

Design of Intervention

Three-Five's leadership expressed a strong preference for a performance-based system, and our design was therefore based on actual data throughout. To guide the process, we assembled a management advisory board consisting of senior leaders from engineering, manufacturing, systems, human resources, and finance, and established a regular meeting schedule during which objectives were set and progress reviewed. The advisory board developed the following as its mission or charter statement:

- Create a system to develop leadership in support of the Three-Five Systems strategic plan.
- Develop a strategy to institutionalize core values and operational principles, and communicate them to functional managers along with expectations.

This charter statement governed all board activities throughout the project. The project was to be performance based, comprise a systematic approach, and be consistent with and in support of the company's strategic plan.

The advisory board would look not only at training but also at the other elements of the human resources system, which figure 1 shows, to determine what contributes to appropriate leadership performance.

Figure 1. Elements of the HR performance systems.

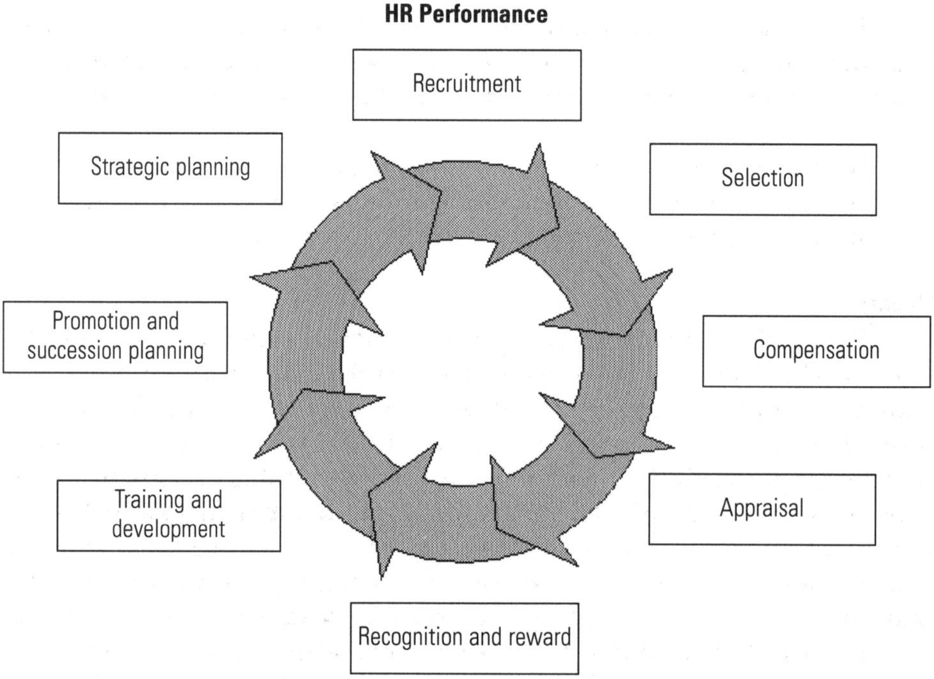

HR Performance

Recruitment

Strategic planning

Selection

Promotion and succession planning

Compensation

Training and development

Appraisal

Recognition and reward

Company Vision, Mission, and Values

Some preliminary steps were required before beginning the actual training and development process. To ensure that our project was consistent with the strategic direction of the company, the senior staff revisited the company's vision and mission statements to see if they were still appropriate. The vision and mission statements would in turn be used to form value statements specific to Three-Five.

Vision

The senior staff made very minor changes to the statement. The statement is, as follows:

> Be the leader in creating and delivering state-of-the-art display technologies which are cost-effective and enhance society's ability to access greater amounts of information.

The vision clearly captures the company's competitive drive, emphasis on high technology, state-of-the-art products, and concern for efficiency in cost and operation.

Mission

The mission, a more concrete charter statement, clearly defines the financial goal, the type of product and customer, and the strategy for achieving shareholder value and customer satisfaction:

> To enhance shareholder value by bringing advanced display technologies to our OEM customers and acting as a seamless extension of their engineering and manufacturing functions.

Values

The advisory board next set about drafting statements that would express the company's values and general philosophy. These value statements derive from the vision and mission statements. The board looked first at value statements by a variety of major American corporations, particularly those of other high-technology companies and those with rapid growth. The advisory board members developed statements, which the executive staff reviewed and approved. Substantial discussion revolved around the concept of employee value to the company and how best to express management's commitment to employees.

The final value statements, which follow in order of priority, reflect the company's belief that dedication to customer success is paramount for a healthy company climate, but that customer success ultimately depends on satisfied, successful employees and a creative, innovative, and ethical environment.

- Customer success is our primary focus.
- Innovative technology enables our customers' success.
- Creativity and continuous improvement in all aspects of our business ensure our success.
- Our customers' success begins with our employees' success.
- Financial health enables us to invest in the future.
- We will act ethically and responsibly, always.

The advisory board next sought to operationalize these values by identifying the activities that characterized each and stating them in behavioral terms. After substantial discussion, they reached consensus and created examples. They later used these data with other input to create performance objectives.

Project Objectives

Following the completion of the work for vision, mission, and values, the advisory board approved the overall project plan, which appears in figure 2.

Figure 2. Overall project plan.

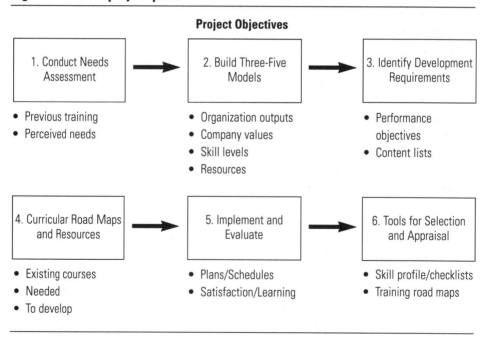

As the consultants, the authors' first and essential step was to gather data from the population to determine what previous training the leadership had received in their previous companies. This task would involve developing data collection tools and a process for analyzing the information gathered. We also needed to understand training requests, what the leadership team perceived themselves to need in the way of training.

After collecting and analyzing the data, we needed a database to establish leadership training records and a tracking system. We would build on the training records system that Three-Five had already begun.

The next step, according to the plan, would be the creation of performance models for leadership that detailed precisely what competencies, skills, and behaviors the Three-Five leadership team desired. From these models, it would be necessary to create performance objectives that tied together the stated company values, strategic direction, and performance requirements identified in the models. The objectives could be the elements of comparison with existing courseware from community educational institutions, private vendors, and current Three-Five presentations and courseware. When we had identified what could be adopted or adapted for our use, we would have a clear idea of what needed to be developed to fill any gaps.

Because we wished to empower individual managers and employees as much as possible, we would create resource guides to spell out training courses, developmental programs, and other aids that could assist employee growth and development to meet the requirements stated in the model. Part of this task would involve creating high-level training road maps specifying the training or developmental experiences required, and the sequence in which they should be taken.

It would be necessary for us to develop an implementation plan, consisting of schedules for selected training courses, a plan to develop needed training to fill any gaps, and a system for evaluating our results. The decision was made to include Level 1 (reaction) and Level 2 (learning) evaluation methods, and to consider the need for Level 3 (impact of performance on the job) at a later point, according to Kirkpatrick's (1994) evaluation model.

As a last step, we would need to ensure that elements of the leadership models were available to the leadership staff, recruiters, and other human resources personnel in the form of job aids to make sure that the process supported the performance specified in the models for selection of future key hires. We knew also that it would be necessary to review compensation, promotion, and award and recognition policies to ensure that all these elements of the overall system were consistent in support of the new model.

Needs Assessment

The advisory board identified its priorities for leadership training as an interim step, and sources were found to meet these needs. In addition, we created a general survey form for everyone in a managerial or supervisory role. The survey asked information on training history and perceived training needs. We compiled the information from the surveys into tables and submitted it to the advisory board for comments and action. To clarify requests and histories, we conducted random interviews with some managers. The results of surveys and interviews confirmed that previous leadership training varied widely, depending largely on managers' former companies. A large segment of the population had little or no training in areas that the advisory board viewed as crucial, including motivation and retention strategies, negotiations, conflict resolution, and finance. We later compared these data to the requirements specified in the performance model and compiled in the plan for curricular road maps.

A sample of the data summary from the needs assessment appears in table 1.

We also gathered information on previous technical training, business degrees, and other relevant data that would assist us in developing a quality curriculum. We were then ready for the next step.

Developing a Leadership Performance Model

The advisory board needed to determine what constituted competent leadership at Three-Five Systems and to provide enough detail to specify what solid performance and skill levels should be. The board reviewed development models from several successful companies and then used facilitated group process to create a modified Rummler competency model (Rummler & Brache, 1990). Essentially this involved identifying key outputs or accomplishments of functional areas and working backward to identify the competencies required to execute them.

When the competencies were identified and prioritized, we noted how they were currently measured (what formal or informal indicators existed for success or failure), and any standards in use.

Table 1. Leadership training history.

Program (Title/Subject)	Participant	Completed (Date/Location)
1. Strategies for employee retention and motivation	Only:	
	Vince	1990 Rosemount
	Chuck	1993 Honeywell
	Henning	1994 MBA
	Pete	1968-1971 Waring Products
	Ed	1976 Hughes Aircraft
2. Coaching/mentoring	Vince	1990 Rosemount
	Liz	N
	Carl	N
	Tom	1986 GenRad
	Chuck	1992 Honeywell
	Harry	1994 TI
	Henning	1990 VDO
	Dean	1995 Honeywell
	Joyce	N
	Fred	N
	Bob	N
	Hallie	N
	Rick	N
	Scott	N
	JDB	N
	Pete	N
	Susan	1996 Dun & Bradstreet
	Ed	1985 NAVCOM Defense
	Makin	N

continued on page 40

We then dissected the competencies to identify component knowledge, skills, attitudes, or attributes. We also identified existing means of providing people with those skills. In some cases, those means consisted of vendor or internal training programs. Other means included presentations, papers, educational programs, or special assignments. Eight major outputs, or areas of competency, were eventually identified for Three-Five Systems. Because of proprietary considera-

Table 1. Leadership training history (continued).

Program (Title/Subject)	Participant	Completed (Date/Location)
3. Conflict resolution	Vince	1990 Rosemount
	Liz	N
	Carl	Micro-Rel
	Tom	N
	Chuck	N
	Harry	1995 Honeywell
	Henning	1994 TI
	Dean	1989 VDO
	Joyce	1995 Honeywell
	Fred	1990 TFS
	Bob	N
	Hallie	1992 Career Track
	Rick	N
	Scott	N
	JDB	N
	Pete	N
	Susan	1968-1971 Waring Products
	Ed	1996-7 Dun & Bradstreet
	Makin	1980 General Dynamics

tions, that list is not presented here in its entirety. An example of one area of competency appears in table 2, although certain data have been deleted to protect the company's privacy.

Identifying Development Requirements

When the performance models were complete, an instructional designer began the process of converting the model data into performance objectives. Most training vendors and educational institutions use performance objectives in the development of their curricula and courseware. Developing performance objectives and pairing them with a comprehensive target population description would enable us to determine matches between existing vendor or institutional curricula and courseware. They would also provide the frame to construct any courseware that we were unable to adopt or adapt to meet our needs. Cost efficiency dictated that we use existing resources wherever possible and keep new development to an absolute minimum.

Table 2. One of Three-Five System's eight competencies.

6.0 Accomplishment/Outcome: The leader will design, build, obtain funding for, and manage the departmental financial plan.

Competency (Ability to…)	Measures/Standards	Knowledge/Skills/Values/Aptitudes
6.1. Understand and manage departmental financial systems within the construct of the annual plan.	• Financial package is met • Actual business plan meets planned business plan	6.1.1 Financial knowledge (P/L Statements) 6.1.2 Internal financial systems (how company accounting system works) 6.1.3. Financial/mathematical forecasting
6.2. Identify and allocate resources, including the projection of needs and the planning process.	• Personal development plan established • Actual achieved by plan • Overtime limited	6.2.1 Resource allocation 6.2.2 Cost-benefit analysis 6.2.3 Planning
6.3. Negotiate and influence senior management, peers, and associates.	• Achievement of plan • Report in Ops Review meetings	6.3.1 Negotiation 6.3.2 Communication 6.3.3 Influence
6.4. Manage within resources; be entrepreneurial within own department.	• Number of task force accomplishments	6.4.1 Planning 6.4.2 Process management 6.4.3 Financial tracking/accountability
6.5. Understand and interpret financial tracking systems; monitor for anomalies and adjust as necessary.	• Financial package reflects requirements of business plan • Monitor variances between plan and actuals • Implement process improvement	6.5.1 Reporting skills 6.5.2 Organization 6.5.3 Financial tracking 6.5.4 Creativity 6.5.5 Negotiation 6.5.6 Cost control

An example of the performance objectives for one accomplishment and competency area appears in figure 3, showing the origins of the objectives in the performance model in table 2. It should be noted that all stages of enactment of the objectives—consultants' development, boards' approval, and the executive staff's approval—were performed with constant reference to the operationalized values of the company and in light of the strategic direction.

Curricular Resources and Road Maps

After developing the performance objectives, the instructional designer identified the best means of meeting those objectives, recommended them to the company, and listed them in a resource guide. Figure 4 shows our general plan for the design and implementation of curriculum materials. We defined the requirements through needs assessment and performance modeling, and stated those requirements by creating performance objectives and a detailed target population description. We used those tools to find resources to meet those requirements. We then produced tools for managers and employees that would allow them to access developmental information and serve as guidelines during performance reviews and performance planning sessions.

Tables 3, 4, and 5 show samples of the resource guide that the consultants created for Three-Five Systems in support of the performance

Figure 3. Performance objectives.

Accomplishment 6.0: The leader will design, build, obtain funding for, and manage the departmental financial plan.

1. Using profit-and-loss knowledge, internal financial system knowledge, and mathematics, the Three-Five Leader will understand and manage the departmental financial systems within the annual plan as indicated by meeting the requirements of the package and actual financials meeting the plan.

2. Using resource allocation, cost-benefit analysis, and planning skills, the Three-Five Leader will identify and allocate resources including projections and planning as indicated by personal development plan establishment and actuals meeting the plan.

3. Using negotiation, communication, and influence, the Three-Five Leader will negotiate and influence senior management, peers, and associates as indicated by achievement of plan and reporting in ops reviews.

4. Using planning, process management, and financial tracking, the Three-Five Leader will manage within resources as indicated by task force requirements met and plan meeting actuals.

5. Using reporting, organization, and financial tracking, the Three-Five Leader will understand and interpret financial tracking systems to monitor for abnormalities and adjust as necessary as indicated by financial package meeting business plan and monitoring variances.

Figure 4. The curriculum process.

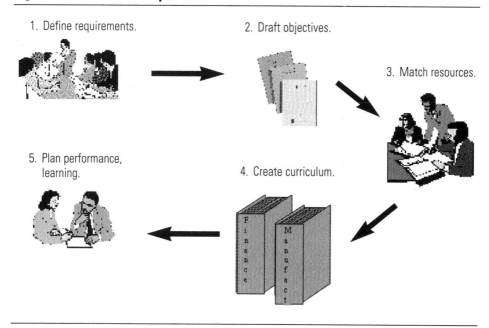

1. Define requirements.

2. Draft objectives.

3. Match resources.

5. Plan performance, learning.

4. Create curriculum.

model. Table 3 shows a portion of the introductory section. Table 4 shows a portion of a resource guide page that correlates to the performance model and objectives in previous examples. Some data have been deleted to preserve the company's privacy. The resource guide was designed to guide performance appraisal and other developmental activities for leadership employees.

Because of Three-Five's position as a high-technology company, employees for the most part possessed sophisticated technical backgrounds, including a working knowledge of both the company's internal intranet and the external Internet, or World Wide Web.

For that reason, we planned from the beginning to place all curricular materials on the company's intranet and included in the resource guide a listing of relevant Web sites for their reference, as table 5 shows.

Tools for Selection and Appraisal

Because we created the resource guide for managers, we included in it tools to guide interviews and selection of candidates for leadership positions, as table 6 shows. These tools were grounded in the performance model and objectives. We produced simplified versions as job aids to assist both the human resource function (recruiting)

Table 3. Introductory pages to the resource guide.

Introduction	
Overview	Three-Five Systems is undergoing unprecedented changes. We have grown by 30% in the past year, our marketplaces have also grown and changed and we have had a large increase in the number of employees in our Company. In response to these changes, we have created an advisory board which includes members from Engineering, Manufacturing, Human Resources, and other disciplines to help ensure that we are developing our leaders appropriately so we can continue to be successful.
Components	The new Leadership Development System we have created includes the following components: • A revised Vision and Mission for Three-Five Systems to take us to the next century • A Leadership Performance Competency Model used to help achieve the Vision and Mission • A Leadership Development Guide to ensure appropriate training and development for the leaders • Training programs for various levels of associates within the Company.
About This Guide	This Leadership Development Guide is designed to assist the leaders and their managers in making the transition to the new leadership competencies created by the Advisory Board. This Guide lists the required competencies to be a leader at Three-Five Systems and the resources available to ensure that you receive the skills and knowledge necessary to complete that role. The Guide describes the entire competency-based system, the new leadership development model, and the job expectations for leaders at Three-Five Systems. This Development Guide also suggests resources that can be used to further develop and enhance skills and knowledge to meet the new competency expectations.

and the leadership team in interviewing and selecting appropriate candidates.

Implementation of Intervention

To ensure successful implementation of the system, we created a custom, two-hour introductory module that Three-Five Systems' own senior management team would teach. The introductory module included the following:

Table 4. First page from Three-Five resource guide with multiple sources for development.

6.0 Accomplishment/Outcome: The leader will design, build, obtain funding for, and manage the departmental financial plan.

Performance Objectives:	Readings:	Developmental Experiences
1. Using P/L knowledge, internal financial system knowledge, and mathematics, the Three-Five Leader will understand and manage the departmental financial systems within the annual plan as indicated by meeting the requirements of the package and actual financials meeting the plan.	Hammer, Michael. *Beyond Reengineering: How the Process Centered Organization Is Changing Our Work and Our Lives.* New York: Harper Business, 1996.	Discuss with your work group the potential for sharing or rearranging responsibilities. Research external practices on processes and systems similar to yours. Meet with team to review work processes and brainstorm ways to simplify them.
2. Using resource allocation, cost-benefit analysis, and planning skills, the Three-Five Leader will identify and allocate resources including projections and planning as indicated by personal development plan establishment and actuals meeting the plan.	McConnell, Steve. *Rapid Development: Taming Wild Software Schedules.* Redmond, WA: Microsoft Press, 1996. Miller, William C. *Quantum Quality: Quality Improvement Through Innovation, Learning and Creativity.* White Plains, NY: Quality Resources, 1993.	Benchmark others' best practices. Celebrate incremental goals. Following the completion of a project, hold a session in which all who were involved assess the process, including you as the manager, and make suggestions for improvements for the next time.
3. Using negotiation, communication, and influence, the Three-Five Leader will negotiate and influence senior management, peers, and associates as indicated by achievement of plan and reporting in ops reviews.	Quinn, James Brian. *Intelligent Enterprise.* New York: The Free Press, 1992. Wheelwright, Steven C., and Kim B. Clark. *Revolutionizing Product Development: Quantum Leaps in Speed, Efficiency, and Quality.* New York: The Free Press, 1992.	
4. Using planning, process management, and financial tracking, the Three-Five Leader will manage within resources, as indicated by task force requirements met and plan meeting actuals.	Whiteley, Richard C. *The Customer Driven Company: Moving from Talk to Action.* Menlo Park, CA: Addison-Wesley, 1991.	

Table 5. Web site listings.

These Web sites contain links to training organizations and other sites specifically developed for human resource activities. Sites are in descending order alphabetically.

Organization	Web Site
Adult Education Collection at Syracuse University	web.syr.edu/~ancharte/resource.html
AskERIC	ericir.syr.edu/
Atlas Web Workshop	ua1vm.ua.edu/~crispen/atlas.html
Big Dog's HR Development Page	www.nwlink.com/~donclark/hrd.html
CMC Information Services	www.december.com/cmc/info/
Computer Training Network	www.crctraining.com/training/
Consultant Resource Center	www.consultant-center.com/
Home for Intranet Planners	www.kensho.com/hip/
HR Headquarters	www.hrhq.com/
Internet Training Center Training Links	world.std.com/~walthowe/tnglinks.htm
Resources for Internet Training	world.std.com/~walthowe/training.htm
San Diego State University EdWeb	edweb.sdsu.edu/
Syllabus Web Top40 Education Sites	www.syllabus.com/top40.htm
TRAIN—Australian Training Information Network	www.opennet.net.au/partners/bvet/train/topics.htm
Training and Development via the Internet	cac.psu.edu/~cx118/trdev/
Training Net	www.trainingnet.com/
Training Net Magazine	www.trainingnet.com/magazine/magazine.html-ssi
Training Resource Access Center	trainingaccesscenter.com/
TRDEV-L—Training and Development Home Page	cac.psu.edu~cx118/trdev-l/
TRDEV-L—Training Summaries (Pennsylvania State University)	cac.psu.edu~cx118/trdev-l/summary.html
Walt Howe's Internet Learning Center	
Wellness on the Web	
World Economic and Business Development Resources	www.mecnet.org/edr/

Table 6. Three-Five leadership performance-specific behavioral questions.

Establish and Maintain Effective Communication	• Tell me about a time when you had a productive meeting. What worked? Why? • Give me an example of a time when you were in a meeting that was not productive. What was the difference between the two meetings? • Give me an example of a time when you had to plan for a meeting where there were going to be conflicts. How did you manage them? What did you learn to do differently next time? • Tell me about a time when you did a good job of listening to someone. What was the result?
Build and Manage Department Budget	• Tell me about a time when you had to acquire resources for a project. What was the situation? How did you get the funding for it? • Give me an example of when you managed your budget to plan. How did this work?
Engage in Self-Leadership	• What does "balance between work and family" mean to you? How do you practice it? • Give me an example of a time when you used diversity to achieve a goal. What did you learn? • What is your personal self-improvement plan? How are you going about acting on it? • Give me an example of how you demonstrated integrity in a situation. What was the result?

- Three-Five leadership philosophy
- expected outcomes and leadership performance
- the purpose, overview, and flow of the leadership development process (including course sequence)
- the results of the needs assessment and model development.

Instructor's Guide

The tools, including an instructor's guide and a participant's guide, enabled the module to be taught to newly hired managers whenever required. The example in figure 5 shows a portion of the fully documented instructor's guide. As part of the guide, we included instruments that would allow evaluation of the module at Level 1 (satisfaction) and Level 2 (learning).

Participant's Guide

A participant's guide was developed for distribution to the leaders, managers, and supervisors who would be attending the introductory module. This guide explained the history and purpose of the project

Figure 5. Instructor's guidelines.

Overview:	Three-Five Systems is implementing a new Leadership Development Program to help the leaders in the Company achieve the revised Vision, Mission, and Values statements. The Leadership Development Model will present an ideal leader with specific competencies and expectations to be met by leaders in the Company.
	The development program consists of several parts. All parts will be discussed in the workshop.
	These new Vision, Mission, and Values statements were written by the Executive Staff at Three-Five Systems and operationalized by the Management Advisory Board. This team also developed the leadership model and these materials.
Workshop Goal:	Participants will leave this workshop with the commitment, skills, knowledge, and enthusiasm to achieve the new Vision, Mission, and Values statements by implementing this Leadership Development Program.
Proposed Audience:	Leaders, Future Leaders, and Human Resources Personnel at Three-Five Systems.

and various types of information designed to facilitate acceptance of the project. The guide included an annotated copy of instructional materials used in the class. An excerpt appears in figure 6.

Other tools, including the development of an instructor's qualification checklist and additional materials for compensation and performance management, were under development as this case went to press.

Full implementation of the project began in the early spring of 1998, with the establishment of training schedules and the evaluation plan with the tools for that purpose. We will be publishing outcomes of the implementation and evaluation and resulting recommendations at the conclusion of the project.

Questions for Discussion

1. Consider the relationship between corporate culture and leadership behavior. What implications does this relationship have for managerial and leadership training programs?
2. What other methods of analysis might have been appropriate for this scenario?
3. What cost-benefit factors should be considered for the development or selection of leadership training programs? Identify the trade-offs for a large company versus a small company.

Figure 6. Excerpt from the participant's guide.

This workshop has been developed to give you, the leaders at Three-Five Systems, an overview of the new Leadership Development Program we are implementing. The workshop will cover the new job expectations, the behaviors we expect of the leaders, how to use the development guide, and how Three-Five Systems will support you in this new leadership role.

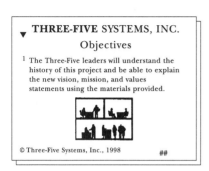

▼ **THREE-FIVE** SYSTEMS, INC.

Objectives

1 The Three-Five leaders will understand the history of this project and be able to explain the new vision, mission, and values statements using the materials provided.

© Three-Five Systems, Inc., 1998   ##

4. What factors must be considered in the transfer of the leadership program or programs to the Philippine plant? What kind of analysis is appropriate to ensure a proper fit and appropriate outcome?

5. As Three-Five Systems grows and matures, what additional steps would you recommend for the institutionalization and maintenance of its leadership programs?

The Authors

Jeremie Hill Grey is a former training manager for high-technology companies, including Intel, Singer Aerospace, and Motorola Semiconductor. She received her doctorate in educational media from the University of Arizona. Grey has 20 years of professional experience in training and development for business and industry, including curriculum design and development (especially competency-based curriculum), instructional design and development, training administration, and documentation and publications. She is now a senior consultant for the Learning Consortium in Mesa, Arizona. She can be contacted at the following address: Senior Consultant, The Learning Consortium, Inc., 2017 W. Lobo Circle, Mesa, AZ 85202.

Elizabeth A. Sharp received her M.B.A. degree from the Executive Program at Arizona State University, and has progressed through a series of increasingly responsible positions at Three-Five Systems to become the vice president of corporate relations, which includes responsibility for human resources.

Jennifer Fox Kennedy received an M.S. in instructional systems at Florida State University, where she was a student of Walter Dick and Roger Kaufman. After completing internships at Arthur Andersen and Los Alamos National Laboratories, Kennedy joined first Motorola University and then training in the Semiconductor Product Sector, where she served as an instructional designer. She is the author of competency-based curricula for a variety of functions, including technicians, leadership, occupational health, human resources, and engineering, and was a major contributor to Motorola SPS's development of the competency-based methodology. She is currently a consultant for the Learning Consortium in Mesa, Arizona.

References

Dubois, D.D. (1993). *Competency-Based Performance Improvement.* Amherst, MA: HRD Press.

Hoover's Business Press. (1997). *Hoover's Hot 250: The Stories Behind America's Fastest-Growing Companies,* Austin, TX: Author.

Kirkpatrick, D.L. (1994). *Evaluating Training Programs.* San Francisco: Berrett-Koehler.

Rummler, G.A., and A.P. Brache. (1990). *Improving Performance: How to Manage the White Space on the Organization Chart.* San Francisco: Jossey-Bass.

Improving Performance Through Competency-Based Selection Techniques

Alston Tanks

Marsha King

Alston Manufacturing is a propane-tank-manufacturing firm located in the Midwest. With an employee turnover rate of 92 percent, Alston was losing nearly $1 million annually. This case explores the problem and describes how the organization was able to reduce the turnover rate to 36 percent by utilizing competency-based selection techniques.

Background

Errors in employee selection are costly and time-consuming to correct (Rothwell, 1996). Alston Tanks, a propane-tank-processing firm located in the Midwest, understood this too well, estimating a cost of $1,200 every time an employee joined the organization and then left it within one month. With 300 employees and a turnover rate of 92 percent (largely because of employees who exited the organization within three weeks of their hire date), Alston was spending an astronomical amount of capital on employee turnover. The costs included temporary agency fees, drug screening, paperwork, wages, and other incidental costs associated with the hiring and termination process.

Pat Dougherty, plant manager at Alston, had decided that this problem was a symptom of a strong economy. He often commented that it was difficult to find loyal employees to perform hard physical labor when fast-food chains and retail shops offer similar wages. Two years earlier, he decided to use a temporary agency to perform the

This case was prepared to serve as a basis for discussion rather than to illustrate either effective or ineffective administrative and management practices.

hiring function. In June 1995, after release of a cost-analysis report revealing the cost of employee turnover, Dougherty along with other members of management decided to consult with an internal performance technologist, Andy Roberts, for assistance in solving the turnover rate problem.

Organizational Profile

Alston Tanks (sometimes referred to as the Tanks Division) is a division of Alston Manufacturing, a steel-processing firm with approximately 10,000 employees. It is a nonunion environment that uses profit sharing as the core of its compensation system. For employees to be included in the profit-sharing plan, they must be full time. This is a problem for the Tanks Division. Because a temporary agency does the hiring, Alston Tanks considers the employees temporary and excludes them from the profit-sharing plan. Employees who stay with the Tanks Division long enough can become full time, but the average waiting time is approximately one and a half years.

Job Profile

The work at the Tanks Division is seasonal. The spring and summer months are the peak production months of the year and, unfortunately, they are the hottest. Temperatures in the plant sometimes exceed 100° F, making work conditions miserable. Large fans were installed to alleviate the situation, but most of the employees complained that they only blew hot air around. Most of the positions in the Tanks Division are assembly. Employees stuff cardboard boxes with tanks ranging in weight from 10 to 40 pounds. Depending on the season, an employee may lift from 300 to 600 tanks per day. It is strenuous and exhausting work.

Approaches to Human Performance Improvement

Roberts, the performance technologist, broke down the human performance improvement (HPI) effort into several stages including:
- identification of the problem
- selection of the intervention
- implementation
- monitoring the process
- evaluation.

Identification of the Problem

Roberts had already spoken to Dougherty, the plant manager, who basically told him that the problem was that people these days have no loyalty. They are not willing to stick it out to become full-time employees. Dougherty suggested that raising the wage from $9.00 to $9.50 would solve the problem.

Every time an employee left the organization, human resources conducted a written exit interview. Roberts examined a total of 167 interviews and concluded that wages were not the problem. Out of the 167 exit interviews, only 14 mentioned low wages as the main reason for leaving. The interviews also revealed that many of the employees choosing to exit Alston had worked for other organizations for long periods of time. They were looking for employment at Alston because they had been laid off. This led Roberts to believe that loyalty was not a problem.

Next, Roberts spoke to the employees. They complained of the heat, strenuous labor, the long hours, the seasonal work, and the lack of profit sharing and other benefits. They rarely complained about wages. Apparently, with the high turnover rate, the employees left behind ended up putting in about 20 hours of overtime every week. With the overtime, they made considerably high wages for that geographical area. Roberts asked the employees why so many laborers left in the first three weeks of employment. They answered that most people have no idea of what they are getting into. "This is not an average nine-to-five desk job," they explained. The job requires a lot of hard work and patience, but pays off for those who can wait it out. They become full-time employees with profit sharing and benefits, and at that time, their wages almost double.

Roberts decided to meet with Dougherty again. He needed to know more about the compensation system. He asked why new hires remained temporary employees for so long. The answer was that because turnover is so high, the company needs to be certain that employees are going to stay before including them in the profit-sharing system. Every time a new hire leaves the organization within one month of his or her hire date, the organization pays $1,200. Including this group into the profit-sharing system would be detrimental to the compensation system because the full-time employees would have to absorb the cost.

Roberts then looked into the hiring process. He made an appointment with the recruiter for Alston Tanks at the temporary employment agency. She explained the recruiting, screening, and interview process that the applicants encountered. Newspaper ads were the primary vehicle for recruitment, and the application was the screening tool. Agency staff called references and examined work history. Once approved, applicants were hired on the basis of whether or not they met the qualifications from the job description Alston Tanks provided. The job description is as follows: "Manufacturing firm is hiring for three shifts. Work includes heavy industrial labor involving assembly. Opportunity for overtime."

Intervention Selection

Roberts believed he had enough information to start making recommendations on possible interventions. He reached the following conclusions:

- Laborers are not leaving because of wages.
- Laborers do not lack loyalty.
- Working conditions are difficult at best.
- The hiring process has failed to find a good fit between organization and employee.

His recommendations were in two stages.

Stage 1

Due to the complex nature of the job, Roberts believed an outside party could not take ownership of the Tank Division's unique needs. He recommended that the Tanks Division transfer the responsibilities of the hiring process from the temporary agency to that of an internal individual or group in the organization. He recommended that a complete job and task analysis be conducted for each position so that a systematic interviewing process could be implemented.

He also suggested creating a realistic job preview (RJP). The purpose of the RJP is to ensure that the organization and each laborer are a good match by giving applicants an opportunity to witness the realities of the job and, therefore, self-select themselves out of the job if desired (Wanous, 1989). He suggested a stage 1 start date for October 1995.

Stage 2

Stage 2 was to include the new employees in the full-time compensation system on their hire date, eliminating the year and a half waiting period. He suggested an approximate stage 2 start date for the spring of 1996.

Implementation

Roberts met with Dougherty and the other managers on July 5, 1995, to discuss the recommendations. They gave their approval and asked him to proceed with implementing them.

The steps in the implementation plan were as follows:

- Conduct a job analysis to determine the competencies necessary to perform each job.

- Create systematic interviews on the basis of the competencies.
- Work with human resources development (HRD) in developing a training program for effective interviewing skills.
- Designate an internal recruiting, selection, and hiring team.
- Work with HRD in conducting a workshop to train the team how to hire effectively.
- Assume the hiring function.
- Monitor the process.
- Begin stage 2.

The Job Analysis

Job competencies are characteristics of an employee that result in effective or superior performance in a job (Boyatzis, 1982). To create a list of these competencies, Roberts looked at the star performers at the Tanks Division to determine what made them superior. He used several nonrepetitive measures including the following (Zemke & Kramlinger, 1982):

- *Interviews:* Roberts conducted interviews with supervisors and laborers to find out who the star performers were. He then talked to them, their supervisors, and their co-workers to understand what made them the best. Some of the questions he asked the star performers were:
  —Describe a time at work when you performed at your highest level.
  —If you had to train someone to do your job, what are the five most important tasks you would teach them?
  —If you had to hire someone to do your job, what are the five most important characteristics you would look for in a person?
- *Performance appraisals:* He examined the performance appraisals of the star performers to find common threads of exemplary performance.
- *Benchmarking:* He looked at other divisions of Alston Manufacturing to see what characteristics their exemplary performers possessed.
- *Observation:* He observed the exemplary performers on the job. He asked the best employees to show him what made them superior.

Roberts developed a list that he felt captured the competencies of an exemplary performer, and then he broke the competencies into two types:

- *External competencies required to perform a job such as typing skills (ability to type 60 words per minute) or computer skills (must be able to program in C++).* These competencies are usually thought of as tasks.
- *Internal competencies required to perform a job such as communication, teamwork, and enthusiasm.* These competencies are usually thought of as characteristics.

The external skills can be taught or learned on the job. The internal skills are much more difficult to learn, however, so Roberts decided to target those skills in the hiring process. The internal skills are as follows:

- *Adaptability:* must be adaptable to the constantly changing conditions
- *Flexibility:* must be able to change shifts easily, work overtime, and alter existing schedule
- *Enthusiasm:* must be able to maintain an enthusiastic attitude at all times
- *Teamwork:* must be able to be an effective team member.

Roberts gave this list to the star performers and asked them if they thought that it described what it took to be an exemplary performer. They added patience because they felt that it required a great deal of patience to stay with the organization long enough to become an exemplary performer.

The new list of internal competencies required to be an exemplary performer were adaptability, flexibility, attitude, teamwork, and patience. Management approved the list.

Create an Interview Based on the Competencies

For each competency, Roberts wrote a question that was related to the job, focused on behavior, and open ended. Managers asked each applicant all of the questions during an interview. The questions were as follows:

- Question #1 *(adaptability)*

   Tell me about a time when you had to adapt to a new environment. How did you handle the new situation? What specific things did you do to adapt? What was the result? What would you do differently? Why? What would you do the same? Why?
- Question #2 *(flexibility)*

   Explain a situation in your last job where you had to be very flexible with your schedule. What did you do to be more flexible? Was it difficult to be so flexible? Did it bother you? Why? Would you do that again? Why? What would you do differently? How?
- Question #3 *(enthusiasm)*

   Tell me about something in one of your past jobs of which you were very enthusiastic. Why were you enthusiastic? What did you do as a result of your enthusiasm? Would you do that again? Why? What would you do differently?
- Question #4 *(teamwork)*

   Give me an example of a time when you worked on a team. What was the purpose of the team? What was your role? What were the results of the team's effort? What role did you play in the result? What would you do differently? What would you do the same?

- Question #5 *(patience)*

    Describe a situation where you needed a great deal of patience. What did you do as a result? What about the situation was difficult? Why? What would you do differently? What would you do the same? Do you consider yourself a patient person? Why?

    Roberts also created a rating sheet, shown in table 1, to help the interviewers objectively measure the applicant's responses to each competency. The sheet was to be used during and shortly after each interview. Job offers went to the applicants with the highest scores.

Work with HRD in Developing a Training Program on Effective Interviewing Skills

Roberts studied HRD's existing training program, titled Conducting Effective Interviews, and made two minor adjustments. He asked that HRD include sections on conducting realistic job previews and on creative recruiting methods.

Designate an Internal Recruiting, Selection, and Hiring Team

Roberts worked with Dougherty to create a team of individuals that would be responsible for the hiring function. It consisted of six employees, three supervisors, and three human resource professionals.

Work with HRD in Conducting a Workshop

The team went through a one-day workshop that focused on how to hire employees who are the right match for the organization. The six employees learned how to do the following:

- create behavioral, job-related, and open-ended questions
- recruit employees
- give a realistic job preview
- conduct the interview
- secure the best person for the job.

During practice sessions in the workshop, the team used questions created from the job analysis and the rating sheet. The workshop was conducted on September 12, 1995.

Assume the Hiring Function

The team took responsibility of the hiring function as of October 1, 1995.

Table 1. Competency-based interview guide.

Competency	Definitely has this competency	Has most of this competency	Could be trained to have this competency	Does not have this competency and would be difficult to train
Adaptability	4	3	2	1
Give examples of behaviors that demonstrate this competency.				
Flexibility	4	3	2	1
Give examples of behaviors that demonstrate this competency.				
Enthusiasm	4	3	2	1
Give examples of behaviors that demonstrate this competency.				
Teamwork	4	3	2	1
Give examples of behaviors that demonstrate this competency.				
Patience	4	3	2	1
Give examples of behaviors that demonstrate this competency.				

Monitor Process

Roberts worked with each individual to be certain all of them felt comfortable with their new role. He facilitated a weekly meeting to help support the group and to answer questions. He sat in on the interviews for several weeks to ensure consistency and effectiveness. While sitting in the interviews, he noticed that the team members had difficulty giving a realistic job preview. He brought this up in one of the meetings. The members explained that it was difficult to give a realistic job preview because they felt that they were making Alston Tanks look bad. Roberts explained that a realistic job preview was given simply to explain some of the realities of the job, not just the negative aspects of the job. They still had a difficult time with this.

Roberts knew that a realistic job preview was crucial to helping applicants self-select themselves out of the job by allowing the applicants to determine whether or not the job was right for them. He decided to create a realistic job preview video. He contacted Dougherty, who agreed. First, he gathered four Tanks Division employees. Two were new hires, and two were exemplary performers. He worked with Alston's Public Relations Department's video expert to capture the four laborers on tape talking about the realities of the job. They explained what the job was like, what was good, and what was challenging. The video also showed the employees performing the job to allow the applicants the opportunity to see what the job was like. Applicants watched the 15-minute video depicting the job before their interviews. After viewing the video, the applicants had the opportunity to decline the interview.

Stage 2

Stage 2 began in the spring of 1996. As the turnover rate decreased, current employees were slowly integrated into the full-time compensation system. By this time, the waiting period was reduced from 18 to 4 months. As time progressed, new hires were expected to become full time upon hire date.

Evaluation

Evaluation was based on employee turnover rate. From October 1995 to July 1996, the turnover rate went from 92 percent to 36 percent. It was calculated by subtracting the unavoidable separations from the avoidable separations and dividing by the number employed during midmonth. The formula is as follows:

$$\text{turnover} = \frac{\text{separations} - \text{unavoidable separations}}{\text{\# of employees at midmonth}}$$

In October 1995, there were 296 separations and 17 unavoidable separations (15 of the unavoidable separations were due to students returning to school). The number of employees during midmonth was 304. The calculation follows:

$$\frac{296 - 17}{304} = 92\%$$

In July 1996, separations numbered 117, and there were 12 unavoidable separations. The number of employees during midmonth was 294. The calculation follows:

$$\frac{117 - 12}{294} = 36\%$$

In October 1995 the organization lost approximately $335,000 because of employee turnover. In July 1996, that amount was reduced to $126,000. When compared to 1993-1994, the average savings for the months of October through July were approximately $72,000 per month, for an annual savings of $864,000. This figure was calculated by subtracting the average lost in each month in 1995-1996 from the average of loss from the same months in 1993-1994. This figure ($72,000) was multiplied by 12 to get an annual savings of $864,000.

The team believed that the reason for success was that the organization and applicants were better matched. Once interviews were based on the competencies, only 60 percent of the applicants were hired. Also, 12 percent of the applicants declined the interview after viewing the realistic job preview video. Because the employee turnover rate is calculated monthly, continued evaluation of this process is in place.

Questions for Discussion

1. What do you feel will be the long-term effects of the intervention?
2. What other interventions would be appropriate for solving the employee turnover rate?
3. What do you think will happen to employee satisfaction due to the intervention?

4. What concerns do you have with the intervention?
5. How might the turnover rate affect performance?

The Author

Marsha King is a Ph.D. candidate in workforce education at The Pennsylvania State University. Prior to graduate school, King worked for three years in a Fortune 500 manufacturing firm as a human resource generalist. She also spent one year as a systems training specialist for Penn State [University] Great Valley. She is currently working for Penn State as a graduate assistant for the College of Engineering.

King has a B.S. in business administration from Ohio State and an M.A. in instructional systems from Penn State. Her current interests include technology in the classroom, organization development, professional development in higher education, and the Internet as a teaching tool. She can be contacted at the following address: The Pennsylvania State University, 927-5 West Whitehall Road, State College, PA 16801.

References

Boyatzis, R.E. (1982). *The Competent Manager: A Model for Effective Performance.* New York: John Wiley.

Rothwell, W.J. (1996). *Beyond Training and Development: State-of-the-Art Strategies for Enhancing Human Performance.* New York: American Management Association.

Wanous, J.P. (Spring 1989). "Installing a Realistic Job Preview: Ten Tough Choices." *Personnel Psychology.*

Zemke, R., and T. Kramlinger. (1982). *Figuring Things Out: A Trainer's Guide to Needs and Task Analysis.* Reading, MA: Addison-Wesley.

LIFE Restructuring

The LIFE Company

Danny Langdon and Kathleen Whiteside

After years of poor management, a new president took over a division of a large insurance company, which was losing market share and profitability. He knew he had a short honeymoon period in which to turn the organization around. He selected the authors as consultants to aid him because they had a good performance (work) improvement model and could work at all the levels of the organization. They worked closely with him and his management team to define the current and desired state of the business unit, the core processes, and the individual jobs, and to ensure that the work groups completed all the performance improvement in 60 days.

Background

The LIFE Company—a real Fortune 500 company, but to which we have given a fictitious name—provides life and disability insurance products to a wide range of consumers. The division that is the focal point of this case provides insurance to banks, mortgage companies, and finance companies, which in turn provide consumers with long-term financing of cars, boats, and homes. The idea is that the financiers have a vested interest in providing the insurance product because they would be one of the beneficiaries if the loan taker died or was disabled. From the insurance company's side, there was a qualified list of potential clients, a built-in marketing arm, and a specific need for insurance.

For 10 years, this division had languished under the leadership of an executive who paid little attention to ongoing business efficien-

This case was prepared to serve as a basis for discussion rather than to illustrate either effective or ineffective administrative and management practices. All names, dates, places, and organizations have been disguised at the request of the author or organization.

cies and customer focus. No attention was paid to costs, speed of claims payments, or difficulties that either the customers (the banks) had in getting questions answered or that consumers had when submitting a claim. Because the parent company, LIFE, is such a large organization with annual revenues in the billions, a little division with revenues of $200 million was not particularly worthy of attention by senior management.

As long as market share was stable and noises were few from customers, the president of this division was able to send in his annual reports, take his annual bonus, and not spend too much time worrying about his product, company, or obligations.

LIFE paid no attention until market share slipped considerably, from 7 percent to 3 percent, and the executive came to retirement age. In searching for a new president for the division in question, LIFE took a risk by hiring an investment attorney who was going through a midlife change in interests and searching for a turnaround opportunity. Because LIFE had not worried very much in the past about this division, it was willing to let an unlikely person take over. Could he improve market share? Could he reduce costs? Could he reorganize the division? He, too, wondered about all these questions, and with little experience in turnarounds, but with a lot of faith in himself and answers presenting themselves, Andy Jones took over the division that we will call GIO.

Prior to Jones's employment with GIO, he had undertaken a different venture. After 15 years as an investment attorney, he thought he would find providing training to attorneys a good and useful experience. He joined the American Society for Training & Development, read every relevant article and book he could get hold of, and called people who wrote books he thought he might be interested in. Although 15 months of attorney training convinced him that almost any other activity could be more fruitful, he had learned that performance improvement was possible through systematic means.

The Organizational Profile

Following are some key points about the organization:
- *The industry:* Insurance. Located in suburban New Jersey, GIO, a $200 million division, is part of one of the world's largest insurers, LIFE (a fictitious name for a real company).
- *The key product:* Insurance provided to banks and other purveyors of consumer credit to be sold then to their customers at approximately the time they bought a car, a home, or refinanced a mortgage.
- *Profitability:* This division was making a profit of approximately 2 percent per year on revenues of $200 million.

- *The context:* There were 200 employees, many with long service records. Morale was moderate; people knew changes were coming, but had not had a vision of what they might be. The popular perception was that there were 50 job titles among the 200 people, but the human resources systems had not been attended to in many years, so there was no way of really knowing.

Industry Profile

The insurance industry is heavily dependent on clerical work. Relatively little automation has occurred. Credit insurance, which is what this company provides, is one kind of insurance. It is based on the model of life insurance that was developed at the turn of the century for poor working people. Over time the products, marketing, and profitability of insurance have all gotten much more complex, but the basic process remains unchanged. Products are designed, risk is assessed, and prices are determined (underwriting) based on the actuarially determined likelihood of a claim being submitted; insurance products are assembled, approved by various state and federal agencies, marketed, sold, and administered; and claims are processed when submitted. Claims processing still depends on handwritten claim forms coming by mail to the claims processing office. Many pieces of paper need to be assembled to make a claims decision. This kind of insurance can be very profitable, but requires sophisticated marketing to reap its full potential.

The number and types of people required to support an insurance product include many entry-level clerical workers, people who have "grown up" in the business serving as supervisors, programmers, and data management types, financial people who account for and invest the revenues, and actuaries and underwriters as well as marketers and managers of various functions.

Key Players

The job titles, status, and backgrounds of key players in this case are shown in table 1.

Company Profile

GIO has 200 employees. They work in approximately 80 jobs that may be classified as 60 percent clerical, 10 percent management, and 30 percent specialists in marketing, management information systems (MIS), underwriting, claims, and actuarial.

Andy Jones assembled the people in the list appearing in table 1 to do the key work of turning the organization around. The directors

Table 1. Key players in the case.

Job Title	Status	Background
President, GIO	New hire—internal	See above.
Treasurer	New hire—external	Hired by the president for his understanding of how to make insurance products profitable
VP, marketing for GIO	New hire—external	Hired by the president for his expertise in marketing insurance products
VP, actuarial	New hire—external	Talented in using actuarial information for business purposes
VP, underwriting	Internal promotion	Skilled in understanding the risks of various product lines and consumer groups; good at identifying potential problems
Director, MIS	Internal promotion	Skilled in developing new processes and the electronic support of same
Director, operations	Internal promotion	Bright young employee; capable of getting enormous amounts of work done
Director, human resources	New hire—internal	Formerly in charge of hiring and benefits; needed to develop skills in job definition, outplacement, and counseling
VP, accounting	New hire—internal	Brought back from retirement
Content expert	External consultant	Excellent background in finance, reengineering, insurance, and product development
Process consultants	External consultant	Authors of case study; background in HR, total quality management, training, downsizing, and process improvement—experts in performance (technology) improvement

of MIS, human resources, and operations created the core team with rank-and-file members of the major functions. This core team was trained to define jobs, work groups, processes, and the business unit. They spent 30 working days defining all the current jobs and current processes using the case authors' "language of work" model (as described in Langdon's book *The New Language of Work,* published by HRD Press in 1995) in order to develop a clear picture of the "what is" state of the organization. They used these data to define the performance gap that needed to be filled to reach the to-be-defined "what should be" state.

History of Key Relationships

The newly appointed president of GIO made it a requirement of taking the job that he be able to recruit key people for various positions. Within bounds, this was allowed. He had worked with a number of the key people labeled "new hire, external" in the table. The president basically hand chose these people, and they were supportive of him and the work he had set out to do. Although these key people did not know each other well at the beginning, the president was able to create a number of team-building activities, such as dinners and other events. He intuitively understood the importance of having a cohesive team.

Although the remaining 200 employees had been employed for long periods of time, some as long as 35 years, the president made it clear that unless major changes occurred in the business, the division might need to close down. Although there was some denial about the future, the truth had been spoken loudly and often. Employees were urged to bid on other positions within other divisions of LIFE, to examine their retirement options, and to investigate other employment alternatives.

The GIO president reported to an executive vice president of LIFE, who in turn reported to the chairman of the company. The president of GIO was positioned to be supported in his activities, although he was expected to do the work without additional financial support from the corporate entity.

Description of the Initiative

The president needed to cut $20 million of operating expenses for the division to survive. He needed to increase market share over a three-year period and reduce costs by 10 percent within one year. Because the major cost of the business was payroll, it was obvious that the way to achieve the savings would come from downsizing. But because he wanted to have a viable business at the end of the turnaround, and because he believed that historically poor management caused the excess, he wanted to approach the downsizing in a systematic way. At the same time, he took a pragmatic view of the budget to do the work. His position was, "If I am in the business of saving money, I need to be frugal in the money I spend to do so. My team will do the majority of the work themselves. I will hire experts who can lead us into the future, but my team will do the restructuring work."

This approach had the additional benefit of keeping all the parties well informed about all the decisions in the project. It also afforded increased commitment to change, and many of the orientation and training processes occurred during the restructuring. Few doors were kept closed; most discussions were summarized and e-mailed to everyone so that they could keep up-to-date on the twists and turns of the project. Elevator conversation was determined in large group meetings. Thus, the entire division heard the same message from everyone—the president, human resources, and restructure team members. This approach helped to preserve good morale during the reengineering process.

Jones was not an expert in this line of business. So he knew he needed to understand what the current jobs were and what the current processes were. With this knowledge, and with access to fine minds free of historical biases, he was sure he could develop the new structure—in essence, a new business—and make it a winner.

His planning included developing a cadre of dedicated managers, committed to his vision of the future, with the skills needed to move into implementation. He went to the outside for two key resources: an employee with lots of knowledge and experience at LIFE, a background in insurance and finance, and experience in the downsizing and reengineering process. The second resource was the authors—Danny Langdon and Kathleen Whiteside, the restructuring and reengineering team who are partners in the consulting firm Performance International. Langdon's book *The New Language of Work,* had just been published. It provided a simple framework for the team to use to address all of their issues through a common performance model that would answer and align:

- What is the current business unit?
- What is the future business unit?
- What are the current processes?
- What are the future processes?
- What are the current jobs?
- What are the future jobs?
- What is the current organizational structure (that is, what work groups exist)?
- What is the future organizational structure (that is, what work groups exist)?

Key Issues and Events

The president of GIO initiated the project. He understood clearly that his business changes could not be executed without a substantial human resource (HR) strategy in place. He also saw that the HR strategy needed to be grounded in the principles of process reengineering. In his search for a model that would link the reengineering and the staffing and structure in one seamless whole, he found the "new language of work" model. Using that model, he saw that he would not have to begin a separate initiative, after reengineering his business, in order to get the right people in the right jobs. He would not need to go through a downsizing that was only thinly related to the changes in the business. He would not need to keep his changes hidden from view. People could see that the new business process required fewer underwriters, fewer claims personnel, and fewer accountants. They were able to see what the needs were, compare the business's needs to their own capabilities, and if a match was not evident, they could work with the HR department to get situated in another internal or external position.

Jones wanted the initiative to be completed in a 60-day time frame, and had negotiated that date with his management. Table 2 shows the key events.

Target Population

The target population for this initiative was everyone in the GIO division, all 200 employees. No one was untouched: either jobs were eliminated or changed. Reporting relationships all changed as well.

Models and Techniques

The model used for the reengineering effort (phases 1 and 2, described in Table 2) was the new language of work. The techniques included the development of what was called a 10-minute teach, a job aid for reference, master facilitation, and the distribution of copies of the book for reference and edification.

The model was the same for the development of the new jobs and the work groups (organizational structure). The techniques included group facilitation, entry into a computer of jobs modeling, use of an LCD projector to project same, conflict resolution methods, and simultaneous grading of the jobs by the HR department in another room at an off-site hotel.

Two processes in place throughout the engagement were "phone-and-fax" consulting and weekly status meetings with the president, which

Table 2. Key events.

Event	Purpose	Participants	Outcome
Creation of reengineering team	To have internal people devoted to the restructuring	Director, MIS (named project manager); director, operations; director, human resources; VP, underwriting; VP, actuarial	Team named and oriented to the president's vision and mission.
Identification of external resources	To prevent floundering, and to create a systematic process	Reengineering team members	Identification of need for expertise in insurance business and on process reengineering.
Contracting with external resources	To ensure content expertise available as needed	President; project manager	Resources made available for team.
Training of team members	To provide a model to the team for completing its work	Consultants; team; expanded team; president	Expanded team learned methodology; described 10 jobs and two processes in first two-day session.
Project planning	To make the tasks and challenges visible	Consultants; team; expanded team; president	A 60-day project plan that covered the timing for all steps in the reengineering effort.
Project execution, phase 1	Develop maps of current processes	Team	$1 million in savings was identified immediately as current processes were made visible.

continued on page 71

Project execution; phase 2	Develop maps of current jobs	Team	It was thought that 25 job titles existed; 81 were found and mapped. Excesses and disconnects were immediately identified.
Project execution, phase 3	Development of new processes	Team plus consultant for facilitation	Mapping of new processes required outsider to prevent myopia and protectionism; four new business processes to support new business were identified in two days.
Project execution, phase 4	Creation of new jobs	12 key management players	25 jobs created and graded in three days, using the four new business processes as the guiding light.
Project execution, phase 4	Creation of new organizational structure (work groups)	12 key management players	Three management jobs were identified to support the 25 jobs and to support the interface between work groups. Structure designed in three hours.
Implementation	Downsizing of organization to meet new business	Director, HR	90% of displaced employees found new jobs within six months—40% within LIFE; 60% outside the organization.

were dubbed "I can't believe it meetings." In phone-and-fax consulting, the project manager regularly sent artifacts that the team produced to the consultants by fax. The consultants would critique the documents, identify problems and potential problems, and coach the in-house facilitator, who was also serving as the project manager. This "phone-and-fax" technique allowed the consultants to stay in close touch with the project while keeping costs low for the client. It allowed the project manager to learn a number of new skills and to depend on experts to keep him out of deep trouble.

The second technique was built into the project plan. The "I can't believe it meetings" occurred every Friday afternoon. They were designed to ensure that the president did not get too involved, but also that the project could meet its tight time requirements. The project manager, and people he deemed necessary, met with the president each week. Together they would review the progress to date, identify problems, and present the issues, which the team could not immediately resolve. The president sorted out which issues were technical (that is, demanded insurance company expertise) and which were "people" or process issues. He took on the technical issues, provided guidelines or resources to handle the people or process issues, and reinforced the team for their work. The project manager prepped for these meetings with the consultant. On the rare occasions that the president got cranky, the project manager had a wise voice for coaching on that angle as well.

Project Process Description

After all the current jobs and processes had been mapped, the new processes had to be mapped. This required some significant input from the president and the insurance content experts, as well as the new vice presidents of marketing, actuarial, and underwriting and the treasurer. Each of these had the expertise to describe how a portion of the vision could be actualized. This part worked well; it was strategic planning at the process level, and an exciting endeavor for the experts.

However, when the team had made two unsuccessful attempts to describe the new business unit, the president approved bringing in consultants to facilitate. It was clear that the issues were too close to home, and the changes were too threatening for the team to describe the new business unit without an objective, outside facilitator.

The consultants used the following steps in defining the new business unit:

- Determination of the key outputs of the new business unit (which were then compared to the outputs of the current business, making for a great number of ahas!).
- Identification of the consequences of each output, coming to understand the purpose of the business and how it contrasted with the old business.
- Identification of the inputs required to produce each output of the business, creating a list of the resources needed to get into, and stay, in this new business.
- Description of the key processes needed to get the outputs that would allow the business to survive. These processes were then exploded in the next level of detail.
- Articulation of the conditions under which the business is run. Because the insurance industry is highly regulated, and regulated differently in each state, the data generated here had significant impact on the creation of the products the business unit would sell.
- The feedback that would tell the business unit it was doing a good job. Because the original company had limped along for 10 years without being "good" because it had no feedback mechanisms in place, this area was an important one in designing the business unit.

With this GIO business unit map in place, the team was able to design the jobs that would allow the processes to be completed and the business unit to meet its goals. The team was able to finalize its business unit map by itself and to revise the new processes based on the new understanding of the business unit. They were then prepared to work together with a pair of facilitators to create new jobs. These are the steps the team followed:

- Review each new process.
- Identify the outputs of each process.
- For each output, identify the possible jobs required to produce the output, often named functionally, without manager, specialist, or other tags. [Note: It is our belief that much of the understanding of the work resides in the team members. Our task is to articulate in a systematic way that thinking which team members hold. If it is counterproductive, the process holds faulty notions up to the light.]
- Identifying the output the job would produce (suboutput of the process), the consequences the task would achieve, the inputs required, the process to be followed, the conditions to be attended to, and the feedback to be given.

The team then viewed these maps to answer the question, "Would it take one person 40 hours every week to produce this output?" If yes, then the next question was, "How many of these outputs need to be produced to meet the needs of the business?" This then answered the question of how many people were needed in various positions.

If the answer to the first question was "no," then we found another output that a person could logically produce in a 40-hour week. This process continued until there was a complete, full-time job. In a few instances, it was clear that a single output could not be combined with others, and we defined these as part-time jobs.

The facilitator posted the job maps on the walls at the same time that they were being entered into a computer. Once agreement had been reached on the job description, it was handed over to two compensation specialists from corporate human resources who graded each job.

At the end of three days, the team had described, written, and graded 25 jobs, and it was exhausted. Entry-level skills and performance expectations were able to be inferred from the work product, allowing posting of jobs and selection to begin within days of the activity.

Figure 1 shows a sample business unit and process work diagram that the team defined in the 60-day time frame. It is similar to work diagrams for work groups and jobs.

Results

The authors prepared a slide show that allowed the president of GIO to present the results of the reengineering to LIFE's sponsoring executive vice president and the chairman of the board. The total number of different jobs needed to support the endeavor was reduced from 81 to 25, and the total number of employees was reduced from 200 to 125. Costs went from $20 million to $12.5 million with this reduction. (Those numbers reflect the cost of their pay, benefits, and support in terms of equipment, real estate, supplies, software, and the like.) An additional $2.5 million was found in the early changes to the process. Claims costs and litigation costs were able to be cut dramatically as well because the process was so lean that mistakes were rarely made. Particularly significant was the focus on restructuring the work groups, with the newly defined jobs, such that client needs were now to be met at a closer, more personal point of contact on a regional basis. Clients had asked for this, and now would receive it.

Figure 1. Sample business unit and process work diagram.

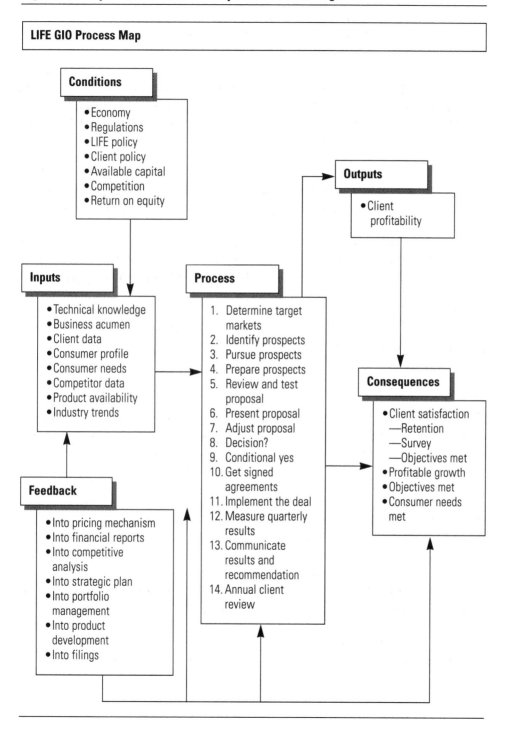

LIFE GIO Process Map

Conditions
- Economy
- Regulations
- LIFE policy
- Client policy
- Available capital
- Competition
- Return on equity

Outputs
- Client profitability

Inputs
- Technical knowledge
- Business acumen
- Client data
- Consumer profile
- Consumer needs
- Competitor data
- Product availability
- Industry trends

Process
1. Determine target markets
2. Identify prospects
3. Pursue prospects
4. Prepare prospects
5. Review and test proposal
6. Present proposal
7. Adjust proposal
8. Decision?
9. Conditional yes
10. Get signed agreements
11. Implement the deal
12. Measure quarterly results
13. Communicate results and recommendation
14. Annual client review

Consequences
- Client satisfaction
  - Retention
  - Survey
  - Objectives met
- Profitable growth
- Objectives met
- Consumer needs met

Feedback
- Into pricing mechanism
- Into financial reports
- Into competitive analysis
- Into strategic plan
- Into portfolio management
- Into product development
- Into filings

Conclusions and Recommendations

Much of the success of the project lay in the hands of the president. He saw his role not as the conductor, but as one of the players in a jazz quintet. Unlike an orchestra conductor who is trying to make the notes on paper sound beautiful and as planned, his task was to make beautiful music. The exact outcome was not always clear, but with good talent and communication, something gorgeous could be produced. His selection of a model on which to frame discussion and outcomes, while reducing emotional ties, and consultants who were compatible with him was a critical step in the success of the project.

The participants in this project, the team, experienced growth on many levels. Rarely had they worked so hard, producing so much in such a short period of time. Because everyone was involved, the approach also allowed for much of the orientation and learning of the new process and structure to occur during definition, as compared to most restructuring where the outcomes are imposed afterwards on those effected. Because of the president's conscientiousness, they were comfortable that people would be treated with human dignity in the entire process. This allowed them to make decisions and recommendations for new jobs that were very much in keeping with individual's needs. Many of the players moved on to new jobs, some in new organizations, that suit their personal and professional goals more closely. Several are using the model in their current settings. It was particularly heartening to see the HR professionals embrace a new way of defining, restructuring, and communicating work.

As consultants, we learned that our model needed to include some additional parts. We have subsequently added the following to the new language of work:
- Standards (What will the work rise to?)
- Support (What needs to be in place for the work to get done?)
- Noise (the articulation of the attitudes and behaviors—including managerial incompetence, racism, sexism—that prevent good work from being done).

Questions for Discussion

1. What was the role of the president of GIO? How did his presence help or hinder the process? Could the same work have been done with a person at a lower level?
2. Why is "rapid analysis" important in business today?
3. What are the disadvantages to such a speedy reengineering process?

4. What is this "new language of work"? What are its key characteristics? How does it allow for alignment of work elements at all levels (business unit, processes, work groups, and individuals) of the business?

5. What are the linkages between business process reengineering and the work of the HR professional?

6. Why did the client find the new language of work important in this project?

7. Describe the role of the HR director in this project. Was it a progressive role?

8. Discuss the use of consultants in this project. What are the relative advantages and disadvantages of the phone-and-fax type of consulting? Why use both external process consultants and content consultants?

The Authors

Danny G. Langdon is a consultant in work systems, instructional design, and performance improvement systems. He is the author of five books in the field of instructional and performance technology, has chapters in eight other books, and has published several articles. He is revising *The New Language of Work,* which is scheduled to be published in 1999 by Jossey-Bass. He is a past international president of International Society for Performance Improvement and has received three international awards from the society for innovative contributions to the field of performance technology. He is a founding partner of Performance International, in Santa Monica, California, which specializes in the language of work approach to business improvement of jobs, processes, work groups, and business units. He can be contacted at the following address: 1330 Stanford, Suite D, Santa Monica, CA 90404.

Kathleen S. Whiteside, partner in Performance International, has more than 20 years' experience in human resource development, instructional design, management development, and organizational development. She specializes in the implementation of such interventions as organization development, job modeling, work group alignment, documentation, personnel policies, selection systems, and performance appraisal. Her experience includes work as an internal consultant with New York Bell, Dayton-Hudson, Prudential Life Insurance, and The Detroit Medical Center. She has been adjunct faculty at the University of California-Santa Barbara and a faculty member at Wayne State University and The Detroit College of Business. Whiteside is co-editor of the forthcoming book *Resource Guide of Performance Technology Interventions.*

You Can Teach Old Dogs New Tricks—You Just Need Different Methods

Harley-Davidson

Curtiss S. Peck

The performance coaching techniques used in sports are transferable to business settings. The following case demonstrates the utility of assessments and performance coaching in a situation where many other techniques had failed to yield a change in behavior. The emphasis is on identification and clarity of causes, coaching, and follow through. The results have been a complete turn-around of a long-term employee who likely would have been terminated.

Background

One definition of insanity is continuing to do the same things and expecting to get different results. So it goes with trying to change behavior that is not acceptable, appropriate, or effective. Some people rely on fear or incentives. Why not, they have worked in the past. Some expect that attending workshops will certainly do the trick. Some will even ignore the behavior, hoping that it will go away over time. More enlightened people will try coaching, but fail to be specific or identify the causes of the existing behavior.

The central figure in this case experienced all of these interventions, but his behavior did not change. The situation became so serious that the management team discussed terminating his employment. This case describes an assessment and consultative approach that clarified the reasons for the behavior and resistance to change, heightened the person's awareness of the impact his behavior was having on others, and offered alternatives without compromising his values or per-

This case was prepared to serve as a basis for discussion rather than to illustrate either effective or ineffective administrative and management practices. All names have been disguised at the request of the author.

sonal needs. The identity of the company is accurate. However, the identity of the individuals are disguised so continued efforts to effect deeper changes beyond this individual are not compromised. The richness of this case remains.

Tom Lewis, the subject of this case, is 56 years old with a 32-year work history with the company. Lewis is an engineer whose opinions have been sought after for many years. His shortcomings include the lack of good leadership, failing to confront substandard performance in a direct and timely manner, performing tasks that are the responsibility of others, failing to complete his job responsibilities on time, and failing to respond to the feedback of his managers. His behavior was tolerated or ignored in the past for a number of reasons. One reason was that Lewis's colleagues consider him a nice person, with a long history with the company, who has made valuable contributions in the past. His value remains today. However, previous managers were reluctant to address his behavior. Others addressed Lewis's behavior, but he ignored their opinions or changed his behavior until the pressure was removed. Lewis attended many training classes, but never developed action plans that he was held accountable for. Previous managers offered incentives, which Lewis gladly accepted. When his behavior became disruptive enough, they used various forms of fear, most of which he ignored.

The turning point came when Robert Percell, the director of manufacturing, asked the author to intervene. This was not the first time Percell had referred an employee to the author. In fact, Percell had also participated in a similar process, but not as intense as the one described below. Percell indicated that he did not want to terminate Lewis, partly because of the value Lewis brought to the company and partly because of Percell's personal commitment to exploring all possibilities to help someone change.

Organizational Profile

Harley-Davidson is an exciting company. There is a mystique about the success of the company and a degree of prestige associated with being a "Harley rider." The company continues to experience tremendous demand for its motorcycles, resulting in the need to increase production capacity. In the past, the powertrains (engines and transmissions) were manufactured in a single facility in Milwaukee and then transported to the assembly plant in York, Pennsylvania. To meet the increased demand, Harley-Davidson purchased a plant from Briggs & Stratton near Milwaukee and converted it into a state-of-the-art powertrain facility. The company has also built a second assembly plant in Kansas City. Much of engineering has moved to another state-of-the-art building, the Willie G. Davidson Product Development Center.

Customer demand drives some of the changes. Other contributing factors have been the increase in look-alike motorcycles. Other motorcycle manufacturers decided to capitalize on the popularity of Harley-Davidson motorcycles. In 1997, there were approximately 36 models from other companies that looked almost identical to Harley-Davidson motorcycles. Some manufacturers have even tried to recreate Harley's unique sound.

Along with the growth and need to remain competitive comes the need for new and additional skills. Many new people have been hired. Some came from other motorcycle companies, some from the automotive industry, and some have had no experience in the manufacturing of motor vehicles. In some cases, people from outside of Harley-Davidson were hired to fill middle- and senior-level management positions. From a business management point of view, most of these hiring decisions made sense. From a cultural perspective, these decisions placed a strain on the company. Many of the "real Harley employees" had been with the company during some very difficult times. They were part of the company when AMF owned it. After the leveraged buyout from AMF in 1981, the company was not doing very well. The company was reorganized and downsized. Those who remained were asked to take pay cuts. A certain camaraderie exists among the people who made those sacrifices during the early and middle 1980s. Some of these "real Harley people" have commented to one another that the new people joining the company had not paid their dues, so why should they benefit in the same way from the present success. In addition, the need to compete with other companies and the skills needed to operate the new facilities require new skills. Over time, most of the Harley-Davidson employees embraced the changes in skills and knowledge needed to perform more effectively and efficiently. Harley-Davidson has been very supportive of training to ensure employee and company success. Under the most recent leadership of now company chairman Richard Teerlink and CEO Jeff Bleustein, the company fosters opportunities for all employees to develop in their careers and experience a sense of job security. Although the company is not perfect, it tries to operate under these strong common values:

- Tell the truth.
- Be fair.

- Keep your promises.
- Respect the individual.
- Encourage intellectual curiosity.

Employees with shorter employment histories have come to Harley-Davidson from companies where the same values were only words on a plaque and not part of the true operating values of a company. All new Harley-Davidson employees go through an orientation that emphasizes these values. However, as the newer employees become more involved in the need for sustained growth and process innovations required to compete globally, the natural tendency is to discard older ideas and ways of doing business. From a Darwinian perspective, this could include the process of natural selection, or survival of the fittest.

The Intervention

The author began the process by formulating questions that might help him avoid some possible land mines.
- What would be the impact of terminating Lewis's employment?
- What are the desired behaviors?
- How much more time, money, and energy should go into salvaging Lewis?
- Does Lewis want to remain employed with the company and why?
- What would be some indicators that Lewis is or is not responding appropriately?
- If everything else has been tried, what could be done that might yield different results?
- How much time is available?
- Is this a political issue?

As difficult as it may be, it is always important to seek solutions that are right for the company and the individual.

Percell indicated that he had a very serious conversation with Lewis about his future with the company. Lewis's behavior either needed to change, or the company would move toward terminating him. Percell asked Lewis if he was willing to meet with an outside consultant who had been helpful to others in the past. Lewis agreed to meet.

Not knowing a lot about Lewis, the author chose to do more fact finding and work on gaining Lewis's trust. He selected a neutral location at the plant for the meeting. It was a small conference room with no distractions. The author shared an overview of his experiences with others at Harley-Davidson over the years.

The author told Lewis that two principles would guide their interactions. First, the author's role is to identify Lewis's strengths rather than his weaknesses. Second, anything Lewis shares will be held in strictest confidence and will only be shared with others with Lewis's permission. The author's two goals are to earn Lewis's trust and offer coaching that will lead to new behavior that is win-win for Lewis and the company.

The author then asked Lewis to share his understanding of the author's role, the nature of the situation, and his desired outcomes. The author has found it beneficial to discuss and clarify these issues up front in every intervention. By asking these questions in the past, the author discovered that individuals were under the misperception that their employment was contingent on his observations and decisions.

This is not and should never be the role or responsibility of the change agent in these situations. False assumptions like these usually negatively affect the interventions and cause the individual to behave in artificial ways. Then, rapport and trust remain absent, resulting in ineffective interventions or unsustainable behavior changes, or both. Also, legal implications emerge in the event the employee is terminated in the future.

The author asked Lewis to share his perspectives on the reasons that led to the author's involvement and what he would like to see as the outcomes. Often, the client tells personal information that can help the consultant understand the individual, his or her sources of motivation, and potential barriers. In this case, Lewis seemed very open. He shared information about his work history, education, problems and successes during his tenure with the company, and family issues. Lewis also freely shared information about personal health problems, some of which were very serious. Lewis was not receiving psychological counseling, nor was he taking any medication for nonphysical problems. He seemed very open and willing to talk about himself and his needs. He seemed to be genuinely looking for someone who would be nonjudgmental—someone he could confide in.

The author is a strong believer in offering people options, along with clear consequences, and letting the individual or individuals make free and informed decisions about their future. There are generally three options available for every situation, occasionally more. In Lewis's case, one option would be to continue as he had in the past. If he did, the consequences would likely be less than ideal (in Lewis's mind).

Choosing this option transfers control of one's destiny into the hands of others. A second option is to leave the company, but to do it voluntarily. The consequences include the possibility of outplacement services, the possibility of a change in compensation (increase or decrease), and the individual's maintaining control of his or her own destiny. A third option is to remain with the company, but to consciously and intentionally change one's behavior. When done properly, the consequences can include a greater awareness and satisfaction of personal needs while improving performance. The third option is also intended to allow an individual to maintain control of his or her destiny.

To facilitate positive change, Heckler suggests, "The first step is to recognize what is, and then to see what is missing, what is out of balance. Then one must interrupt the old pattern. This evokes a startle response, which in turn creates an opening and excitement to work with. Then the person is given new forms and exercises to practice and use in the newly opened space" (1993).

The Theory

To interrupt old patterns of behavior, one needs to know the underlying causes of those behaviors. An approach the author has used successfully many times in the past is based on the theory of attentional and interpersonal style, which Robert M. Nideffer developed in the early 1970s and which athletes, elite military units, and businesses continue to use today. Following is an overview of the theory. For an indepth coverage, please read the works of Nideffer (1993).

In summary, the theory of attentional and interpersonal style assumes that:

1. Human beings have attentional and interpersonal characteristics that have both state and trait components.
2. Given the capacity for a particular behavior, optimal performance requires attention to task relevant cues and an appropriate level of arousal.
3. There is a mutually interdependent relationship between the level of physiological arousal and attention to task relevant cues.
4. There are four different types of attention, any one or all of which may be required in a given performance situation.
5. Different performance situations make different attentional demands.
6. Different individuals have different attentional strengths and weaknesses.

7. Success comes from finding a performance arena that matches your own attentional strengths and minimizes your weaknesses.

8. Performance differences between "superstars" and the average person can be explained on the basis of:

    a. Different levels of physical and/or attentional skill.

    b. Greater attentional control under stressful conditions.

9. Increasing arousal results in increases in respiration rate and level of muscle tension.

10. Increasing arousal results in a loss of attentional flexibility as the individual relies more heavily on his or her most highly developed attentional ability.

11. Increasing arousal results in a loss of flexibility and/or control over interpersonal needs and behaviors that are directly related to performance.

Attention has both direction and width. There are performance situations requiring attention to one's external environment, as in the case of driving a car, operating a piece of machinery, attending to a group of prospects in a meeting, or investigating a crime scene. Other performance situations require attention to internal processes, including thoughts and feelings. The directional components of attention are depicted on the vertical axis in figure 1.

Attention also has a width component shown on the horizontal axis in figure 1. Width of attention has a range from "broad" to "narrow." There are performance situations that require seeing the big picture and others that require being focused on specific details. Width can be easily demonstrated. After reading these directions, try them. Sit in a relaxed position. Do not focus on anything specific in the room, but instead try to see how many aspects of your immediate environment you are aware of. Do this without moving your eyes. Are you aware of people and objects, including their shapes, colors, relative height, and distance to you? After about 10 or 15 seconds, focus on something specific in the room. Look at the detail. While you are focused on the detail, you lose your awareness of many of the other objects in the room. If you return to a less-focused state and become more aware of your surroundings, you can no longer attend to the details of the object you were previously focused on.

Our ability to attend appropriately to situations and to rapidly shift our attention increases our effectiveness. Some situations require one or two types of attention, whereas others require shifting between three or all four. A broad-external approach to attention allows us to pick up on a wide variety of environmental cues. Examples include facilitating a meeting and driving in congested traffic. When we use

Figure 1. Concentration skills.

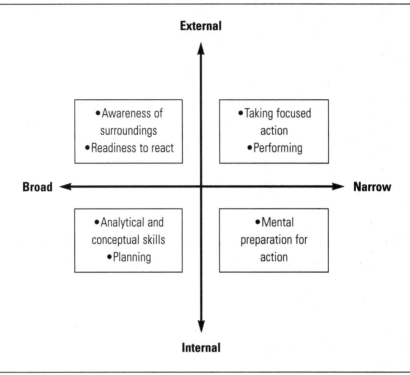

our broad-internal attentional skills, we attend to a wide variety of internal information or cues to organize, analyze, and plan. Examples include problem solving and business planning.

Mental rehearsal is a form of narrow-internal attention—thinking about what we will say or do in a given situation. You are using narrow-internal attention just before you respond to a question. Narrow-external attention is the process of acting or reacting. It is the process of doing or saying the things you thought about or responding to environmental demands.

Heckler addresses the relevance of attentional skills and performance by writing, "Attention is a primary ingredient in embodiment and, at the same time, the connecting thread throughout our learning and development" (1993). The exercise described above demonstrates that attention can be directed. Heckler helps understand the potential importance of this for changing Lewis's behavior when he writes, "The power of directing attention is key in embodying ourselves." The author's purpose was to empower Lewis to voluntarily change, not to manipulate him. The intent was to provide him with new skills to deal with situations differently.

Heckler summarizes the importance of attention and learning when he writes, "Paying attention to what we are doing provides a spaciousness that allows self-inquiry to take place. With our attention, we can literally open ourselves to participate in something that is larger than the boundaries we are normally accustomed to. Through an ongoing practice of paying attention, we can begin to contact an intelligence that is deep enough to be the source of our learning and precise enough to show us how we learn. This awareness is the basis for learning and transformation" (1993).

Learning and transformation require flexibility. However, the excitement and dynamics of specific situations can hinder one's flexibility. Increasing one's level of excitement or arousal can result in a loss of attentional flexibility and control over interpersonal needs and behaviors that are directly related to performance. As arousal increases, it is natural for people to rely heavily on their dominant attentional style and certain interpersonal characteristics.

Figure 2 depicts the dynamic relationship between interpersonal characteristics, arousal, concentration, and performance. As pressure increases in performance situations, our attention tends to narrow. Many people begin to worry, thus getting stuck in the lower-right quadrant (see figure 1). In some cases, they become so stuck inside their heads that they cannot perform, they cannot think of alternatives, and they fail to pick up on things going on around them or verbal messages directed toward them. The more they worry about their performance, the worse it often gets. As performance effectiveness decreases, arousal continues to increase. This cycle continues until something interrupts the process.

Nideffer addresses the importance of understanding the causes of increased arousal levels and the need to control our arousal as a key to optimal performance. "Increasing your ability to understand, predict, and control behavior depends upon increasing your ability to anticipate those factors that will alter a person's level of arousal, and to then be able to anticipate how any resulting changes in the individual's attentional and interpersonal flexibility will affect performance" (1993).

The level of arousal in performance situations is dependent upon a few things: the emotional importance of the performance out-

Figure 2. Relationship between interpersonal characteristics, arousal, concentration, and performance.

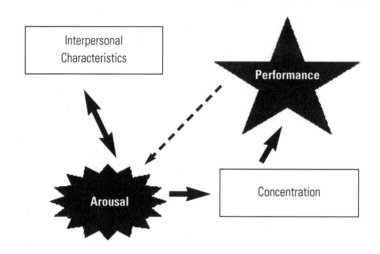

come to the individual, one's self-confidence, and the match between the performer's attentional abilities and the attentional demands of the task.

Interpersonal needs and the dynamics of specific situations can have the same effect on arousal, concentration, and performance. According to Nideffer, those characteristics seen as most important to people (thereby most generalizable across a wide variety of performance situations), include:

- the individual's desire and/or need for control over situations
- the speed with which an individual needs to make decisions (for example, the extent to which the person will sacrifice speed for the sake of accuracy, or vice versa).
- the balance between the individual's need for involvement with others (extrovertedness) and his or her need for personal space and privacy (introvertedness)
- the ability or willingness of the person to express himself or herself intellectually, to speak out in groups
- the ability to express anger, to confront issues, to question critically, and to challenge others
- the ability to express support and encouragement, to be positive.

Nideffer does not see personality characteristics as good or bad (1993). Instead, they need to be thought of in terms of the demands of a particular performance situation. Personality characteristics are only an asset or a liability within the context of a particular situation. For example:

- Most situations either require you to take control, or to give it up to someone else. If you are able to match the situational demands, you perform closer to your optimal level.
- Different situations make different demands in terms of the speed with which decisions are made.
- Different situations make different demands in terms of involvement with others.
- Different situations make different demands in terms of the amount and method of interpersonal expression of ideas, and of negative and positive thoughts and feelings.

Nideffer developed a diagnostic tool known as The Attentional & Interpersonal Style (TAIS) inventory (1996). TAIS is a 144-item self-assessment inventory that measures 18 variables. Six reflect attentional processes, two reflect behavioral and cognitive control, nine describe interpersonal style, and one measures the tendency to be self-critical. Table 1 shows the TAIS scales along with abbreviations for each scale.

Lewis agreed to complete the TAIS inventory. Figure 3 shows the results of his answers in percentile scores. They are a function of a comparison of Lewis's scores with those of the standard population, which is represented by the 50th percentile. Lewis received a comprehensive narrative report that offers interpretive comments for all the scales, along with recommendations. A single scale sheet, similar to figure 3, was used to help Lewis understand the dynamic interactions of the scales.

The high scores for BIT and NAR indicate that Lewis is likely to enjoy playing with information or ideas in his head and then looking for ways to apply them. Also, the high BET score indicates that Lewis tries to shift his attention quickly between attentional styles. He tries to do them all well, and probably does so as long as he's not under pressure. None of the overload scores (OET, OIT, RED) are elevated, which would tend to indicate that when distractions occur, they are likely to be random. However, Lewis's need for information (INFP) is high, and he has some tendency to be impulsive (BCON), which may cause him to overload himself unintentionally.

Lewis has had a history of having his opinions sought after. Despite having attended workshops on project management, delegation, and communication, he has had difficulty delegating and completing some of his work in a timely manner. Lewis's need to take charge

Table 1. List of TAIS scales.

Scale	Scale Description
BET	**Broad-external attention**—High scores indicate good environmental awareness and assessment skills.
OET	**Overloaded by external information**—High scores are associated with errors because attention is inappropriately focused on irrelevant external stimuli, with visual, auditory, or both.
BIT	**Broad-internal attention**—High scores indicate good analytical and planning skills.
OIT	**Overloaded by internal information**—High scores are associated with errors due to distractions from irrelevant internal sources, including thoughts and feelings.
NAR	**Narrow-focused attention**—This is a single scale that addresses both narrow-internal and narrow-external concentration. High scores indicate the ability to remain task oriented, to avoid distraction, and to stay focused on a single job.
RED	**Reduced flexibility**—High scores are associated with errors due to a failure to shift attention from an external focus to an internal one, or vice versa.
INFP	**Information processing**—High scores are associated with a desire for and enjoyment of a diversity of activity. This also tends to indicate a high need for information.
BCON	**Behavior control**—High scores are associated with an increased likelihood of either "acting out" in impulsive ways or a tendency to establish one's own rules rather than strictly adhering to other's, or both.
CON	**Interpersonal control**—High scores are associated with both needs to be in control in interpersonal situations and with actually being in control.
SES	**Self-esteem**—High scores are associated with feelings of self-worth and self-confidence.
P/O	**Physical orientation**—High scores are associated with having been physically competitive and with the enjoyment of competitive activity.
OBS	**Speed of decision making (originally labeled obsessiveness)**—This scale reflects the speed of decision making and worry. High scores are associated with increased worry and difficulty making decisions.
EXT	**Extroversion**—High scores indicate an enjoyment of social involvements and a tendency to assume a leadership role in social settings.
INT	**Introversion**—High scores indicate a need for personal space and privacy.
IEX	**Intellectual expression**—High scores indicate a willingness to express thoughts and ideas in front of others.
NAE	**Negative affect expression**—High scores indicate a willingness to confront issues, to set limits on others, and to express anger.
PAE	**Positive affect expression**—High scores indicate a willingness to express support and encouragement to others.
DEP	**Self-critical**—A high score is associated with situational depression or self-criticalness.

Figure 3. Results of Lewis's TAIS Inventory.

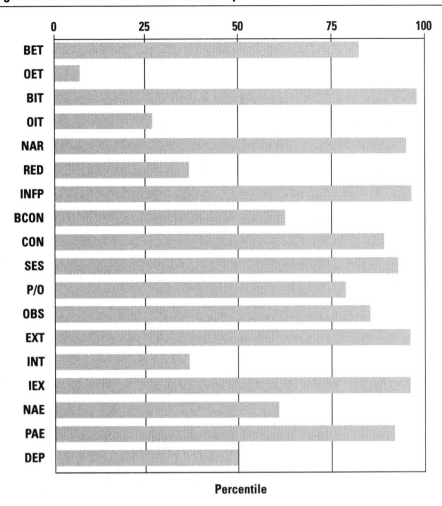

Percentile

(CON) and to be seen as a competent individual (IEX and PAE) are certainly fine qualities. However, when the need for control (CON) and a person's self-esteem (SES) are extremely high (greater than 90), these can be indicators of poor listening skills. Lewis is also not afraid to engage in interpersonal conversations as shown from his high extroversion (EXT) score. He is likely to get most of his energy from others and would have a difficult time being by himself for extended periods.

Interestingly, Lewis has an elevated OBS score, which indicates that he tends to worry about decisions, most likely about topics that are not completely familiar to him. This may be one of the indicators of why he continues to do things that others should be doing (they are familiar tasks) and often fails to complete current assignments without prodding. Even though his NAE score is at the 60th percentile, it is 31 and 36 percentile points below PAE and IEX, respectively. This suggests that Lewis is likely to take an indirect approach when a situation requires direct and timely feedback to an employee about poor performance. Lewis is likely to say that he did talk with the employee, but when asked, the employee is likely to respond that Lewis never talked with him about his behavior.

Lewis received a copy of his full interpretive report. He indicated that it was the most accurate piece of feedback he had ever received. He felt that it pointed out his shortcomings without being judgmental. Based on the report and a one-on-one feedback meeting to discuss the results, Lewis indicated that he thought he had been a team player, but he now realized how he has forced his views on others. "I learned a lot about leadership from football and from having been in the military. There was only one boss. I realize now that I need to change my approach."

Lewis had been doing things for others because he needed to be seen as competent. This created opportunities for others to seek him out for answers. Lewis tended to provide only answers and not the method or information he used to arrive at the answers. This created a sense of dependency, a feeling of being wanted. We discussed his needs for affiliation, power, and achievement. Through a series of questions, he came to the conclusion that he could satisfy his personal needs by asking others questions to help them arrive at their own answers. People would still come to him, not for answers, but for guidance with finding answers. In addition, Lewis is being coached on active listening, ways to confront unacceptable behavior directly and in a coaching manner, identifying barriers to decision making, sharing control, and controlling his arousal levels through centering techniques and attention control training.

In addition to monthly one-hour meetings with the author, Lewis has formal weekly meetings with Percell. Percell uses the TAIS scores, which Lewis freely shared, as a coaching tool. Lewis provides weekly feedback on projects and is able to share any concerns or fears he has about new assignments or loss of social involvement and approval.

Lewis has commented to the author and Percell that for the first time in a very long time, he now feels that his manager understands what he does from day to day, is more realistic about his performance, and is sincerely interested in him.

Lewis continues to respond positively to Percell's coaching. Percell and Lewis continue to use the TAIS results as a basis for understanding how Lewis's needs and skills blend with the demands of the job. Lewis has taken an assertive and direct coaching approach with a difficult employee whom he had avoided in the past. Lewis's employment is no longer in jeopardy, and his level of satisfaction is high. Others who have worked with Lewis have commented to him about his change in behavior. These comments have helped reinforce the new behavior.

Questions for Discussion

1. What were key learning points for you in this case?
2. Why do you believe this intervention worked when others had seemingly failed?
3. What did you like about this approach?
4. What would you have done differently?
5. As you reflect on Nideffer's theory, try to recall a time when your arousal level was so high that you had difficulty thinking of options or taking action in a timely manner. What caused your arousal to increase, and what were the performance outcomes?
6. How will the information in this case study contribute to successful interventions for you in the future?

The Author

Curtiss S. Peck is the president of Assessment Systems International, Inc. He is a registered organization development consultant and the author of several standard multirater 360 feedback assessment instruments. He is the author of a paper titled "360 Degree Assessments: How to Avoid a Disaster." Peck has over 20 years of consulting experience specializing in executive and performance coaching, organization development, employee relations, and developing high-performing teams. He can be contacted at the following address: Assessment Systems International, Inc., 15350 W. National Avenue, New Berlin, WI 53151-5158; or by e-mail at cspeck@execpc.com.

References

Heckler, R.S. (1993). *The Anatomy of Change—A Way to Move Through Life's Transitions.* Berkley, CA: North Atlantic Books.

Nideffer, R.M. (1993). *Predicting Human Behavior.* New Berlin, WI: ASI Publications.

Nideffer, R.M. (1996). *The Attentional & Interpersonal Style Inventory (TAIS)— Theory and Application.* New Berlin, WI: ASI Publications.

Pratt, R.W., and R.M. Nideffer. (1994). *Coaching—Attention Control Training in Business.* Escondido, CA: Enhanced Performance Systems.

Developing Strategic Software Skills in Support of SEI

Motorola Semiconductor

Marilyn Kerr and Jeremie Hill Grey

This chapter describes a major performance improvement project undertaken to support the development of software skills within the traditionally hardware-focused semiconductor products sector of Motorola. The project used competency modeling to accomplish the following:
- *identify and document 18 previously unrecognized software functions*
- *identify performance training requirements for each function*
- *develop training resources to meet the requirements*
- *enable attainment of Software Engineering Institute (SEI) level measurements.*

Background

Founded in Chicago in the 1920s by the Galvin family, Motorola initially manufactured radios and radio equipment, but over the years it has expanded to include the manufacture of computers, cellular phones, pagers, aerospace, and a host of other technologies and products. With approximately 150,000 employees worldwide, Motorola, based in Schaumburg, Illinois, has become one of the largest and oldest of American high-technology corporations. "Chips" manufactured by the Semiconductor Products Sector are the basic building blocks of all of Motorola's products.

The Semiconductor Products Sector (SPS) employs 50,000 engineers, technicians, manufacturing, and support personnel worldwide, and has large-scale operations in Arizona, Texas, California, Virginia, and North Carolina as well as in France, Scotland, Germany, Japan,

This case was prepared to serve as a basis for discussion rather than to illustrate either effective or ineffective administrative and management practices.

Singapore, Hong Kong, China, Taiwan, Malaysia, the Philippines, and many other locations abroad.

In the 30 years since the rise of the semiconductor chip business, intense competition and rapid innovation have resulted in exponential increases in speed, power, complexity, and miniaturization. Traditionally, hardware design had produced technological improvements, but by the late 1980s, it was clear that the chief source of competitive advantage would be software. By the early 1990s, a major Motorola corporate initiative had been undertaken to improve overall software competency. SPS and its component groups, each of which constituted a major business, began execution of the initiative.

The Software Council

The Logic and Analog Technology Group (LATG), headed by Gary Johnson, began an aggressive software campaign. The LATG/East Valley Training & Development group conducted a series of interviews with software subject matter experts early on to determine major training and organizational development issues, and it began the formation of a software education council to support the process. A key question was the definition of the term *software competence*, and how SPS's unique circumstances and performance compared to the SEI requirements. The tremendous scope of the project posed challenges. All job descriptions and promotional matrices were based on traditional hardware models. Software personnel were classified under hardware categories and felt themselves to be a minority, little understood or appreciated. We needed to understand the various software functions and what constituted sound performance in each of those functions.

The early efforts received a substantial boost with the establishment of a groupwide Software Council and associated metrics to track performance. Jan Lamb, LATG organizational effectiveness manager, supported the initial kickoff of the initiative with the management staff to empower the project teams to drive to success. The Software Council consisted of four focus teams consistent with the primary software development areas: computer-aided design (CAD), test, computer-aided manufacturing/computer integrated manufacturing (CAM/CIM), and business. These focus teams, composed of various managers and senior specialists, represented the software practitioners to the Software Council and acted as the execution vehicle for early program deliverables. Motorola's corporate center assigned the quality organization, a department within the company, overall responsibility for achievement of the software quality goals. Johnson named Roger Newkirk, LATG's reliability and quality assurance director, as the sponsor for this initiative, responsible for breaking down barriers impeding progress toward the goals. Glen Cooper was named the full-time software initiative champion, which meant he had responsibility for the execution of the software initiative within LATG and acted as a facilitator for its progress. A key measure of success for this council was identified as the achievement of specified SEI levels for software competency over a multiyear period.

The Software Council developed an action plan to achieve a series of goals, including SEI level achievement. The primary focus areas were the following:

- awareness
- education
- infrastructure
- process
- cultural change
- technology.

The Software Council recognized software education, one of the six focus areas, as a major component for attainment of the other five. To address this area and attain the desired increases in software competence, the Software Council formed the Software Education Council as a subset of it, as figure 1 shows. Key technical representatives from each focus team were assigned to the education council, under the direction of technical project leader and champion Glen Cooper. Marilyn Kerr, an energetic instructional designer, was assigned to support the education council and lead it through the intricacies of building the necessary competency models, coordinating resources, and making the required training a reality.

The team's goal was to create and implement a software curriculum for the software community within 16 months. This situation posed unique challenges. Recognizing that each employee had a unique set of knowledge and skills, team members knew that they couldn't offer one curriculum as university's do and that a list of predetermined courses wouldn't be effective. The software curriculum would need to be flexible so employees could match it to their own skill set and job responsibilities.

Population and Intervention Design

A demographic analysis of the organization's software population identified the total software population of individual contributors and first-level managers and their distribution across business

Figure 1. Software and education council structure.

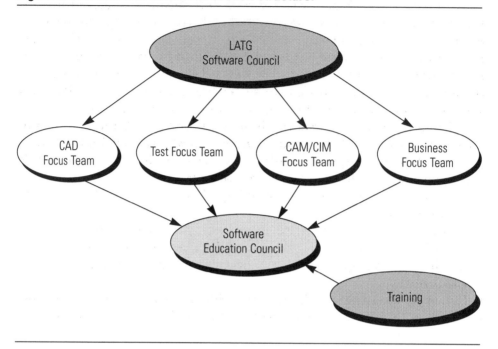

operations. The distribution of the individual contributors engaged in software development activities across software functions was represented as follows:
- computer-aided design, 34 percent
- computer-integrated manufacturing and computer-aided manufacturing, 20 percent
- test systems, 34 percent
- business systems, 12 percent.

The demographic analysis confirmed that most software professionals were not software engineers, but rather hardware engineers performing software duties or system administration tasks. Most of them lacked formal training in software processes, resulting in greater cycle time, decreased customer satisfaction, and poorly developed software as defined by not following good software development processes. Developing an infrastructure and associated tools that could assist in the application and utilization of a professional software process approach was a clear priority for the Software Council.

The Software Council, with the assistance of the instructional designer, mapped the software population to the organizational hierarchy. As a result of this mapping, council members learned that many of the software professionals reported to first-line managers who had hardware engineering backgrounds but little knowledge of software engineering processes. The situation at the next level in the organization was more critical. Only a handful of second-level managers had software engineering backgrounds and appreciation for individuals in the organization who had those skills and ability. These data had serious implications for the organization, as figure 2 shows.

From their interviews and discussions, Software Education Council members learned that many software professionals had software process skills inadequate to allow the organization to reach its SEI level goals. They identified several root causes:

- Most software professionals developed software as only a portion of their jobs.
- Managers without software engineering backgrounds were frequently unaware of the software skills that software professionals needed to develop in order to improve the organization's strategic capabilities.
- Few or no tools were available to help identify software training needs.
- Curriculum had not been developed for software course selection.

Figure 2. Organizational profile.

Reporting Options for Software Individual Contributors

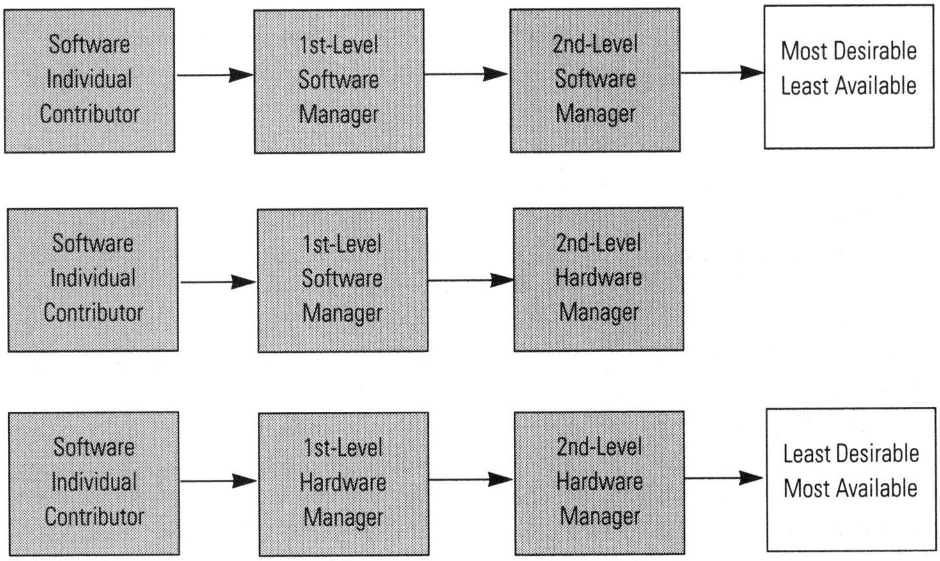

Motorola requires that each employee receive a minimum of 40 hours of training per year. Each year, managers and employees develop individual development plans (IDPs) to guide employees in selection of appropriate courses. When the Education Council reviewed how managers worked with their software employees to create IDPs, it became obvious that inadequate tools existed to guide them through the process. The Software Education Council needed to adopt a strategy for identifying required competencies and tools to acquire them. A software training curriculum was needed. Figure 3 outlines the existing situation and the desired end state.

Because a software curriculum did not exist, or managers did not emphasize building solid software process knowledge, employees frequently enrolled in courses that did not improve their software skills. This practice resulted in wasted time, effort, and money due to inappropriate training. It was clear that a defined process was needed to help software practitioners and their managers complete their development plans. Such a process would explore software competencies, identify individual weaknesses, and provide known courses or interventions to address those weaknesses. As a result, the training needs of both the work group and the individual would be satisfied. With the proper training, marked improvement in software quality could be expected.

Figure 3. Software education flow chart.

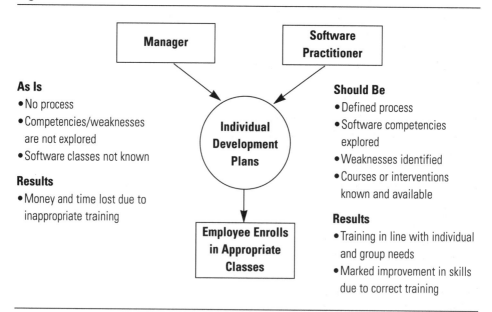

Competency Model Components

On the recommendation of Marilyn Kerr and Jeremie Hill Grey, the Software Education Council adopted the competency-based curriculum (CBC) methodology, developed by the Motorola-wide Competency Task Force led by Robert Aron of Motorola University and used widely by the various training groups of the Semiconductor Products Sector. This approach involves identifying the principal outputs of a functional area and then using a performance model to work backwards to determine the competencies and knowledge, skills, and aptitudes (ksa's) necessary to achieve the required outputs. The team added the use of a Rummler competency model to document one or more of the following: measures, standards, existing training resources, and developmental interventions such as rotational assignments.

Curriculum Development Process

The Software Education Council explored existing curricula to determine what might support the software community. The information obtained showed that nothing comprehensive had been done to date for the software community. Four alternative methods to developing curriculum were examined: DACUM, Rummler competency models, information interviewing, and training road maps. The team dismissed the DACUM process, which typically identifies only general tasks and activities, as lacking the appropriate level of detail required for the SEI effort. The group resolved to combine competency modeling with information interviews of recognized experts, and to produce training road maps (course listings) as part of a resource guide available for managers and employees.

The Rummler competency modeling approach had many advantages, and the group selected it. This approach:

- required consensus
- could identify both the current skills inventory, and paired with contingency planning, the future requirements
- used a structured group process, which in the past had worked well with other technical professionals
- was compatible with many previously developed curricula for other areas.

The curriculum development process included the following steps, which figure 4 illustrates:

1. *Collect data on work products, knowledge and skills, measures and standards.* In developing competency models, the instructional designer held several in-depth group interviews with recognized, outstanding subject matter experts to document existing best practices along with

the necessary knowledge and skills to achieve competence in the respective areas. The data were then fed into the models, which were developed with groups of subject matter experts. The models documented the job functions as they currently existed, but could easily be adapted to include scenario or contingency planning for future competencies and changing knowledge and skill requirements.

2. *Write performance objectives.* The objectives contained measures and standards to determine acceptable performance so that everyone knew what was expected and how the performance would be measured upon achieving the competency.

3 and 4. *Source training resources and interventions to build knowledge and skills.* Multiple training resources provided information, as number 3 in the figure shows. These resources included Motorola University courses, external vendors, universities, and training institutes. The pieces came together in a variety of interventions, including developmental opportunities such as rotational job assignments, literature, and mentoring opportunities.

5. *Publish competency models with a resource training guide for managers and employees.* Publication included both hard copy distribution and Web pages that were accessible to managers and employees.

6. *Train managers and individual contributors to use the curriculum for training planning.* Development of a one-hour introductory workshop helped to ensure transfer and use of the curriculum tool by the software population.

Implementation of Intervention

Implementation included the production of a series of products, an aggressive roll-out campaign involving a workshop, and organizational publicity to support the effort and expedite execution.

Products

The four major products developed for the project were as follows:

1. *Competency models for 18 software engineering and systems support functions.* Each competency model contained a list of high-level accomplishments, the outputs of each software professional's functional area. Each competency model used the accomplishment list for each type of software professional and identified the competencies required to achieve these accomplishments. Figure 5 shows a sample of a completed competency model page.

The models were developed for the following functions:

Figure 4. Curriculum development process.

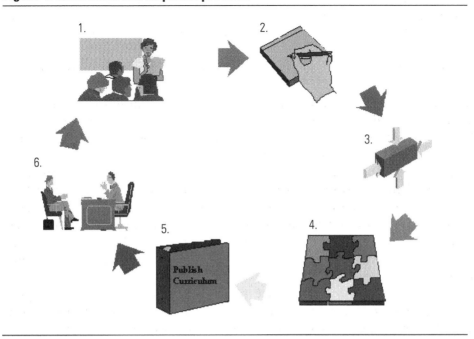

- general software engineer
- business systems analyst
- CAD engineer
- library design engineer
- SPC software developer
- systems engineer
- software test engineer
- configuration management administrator
- data administrator
- database administrator
- information technology security
- network administrator (tiers 1, 2, and 3)
- systems administrator
- software quality assurance engineer
- software engineering process specialist
- case support specialist.

2. *A resource index.* Training specialist Lynn Stephen compiled a comprehensive index of over 500 listings of training selections and

Figure 5. Sample competency model page.

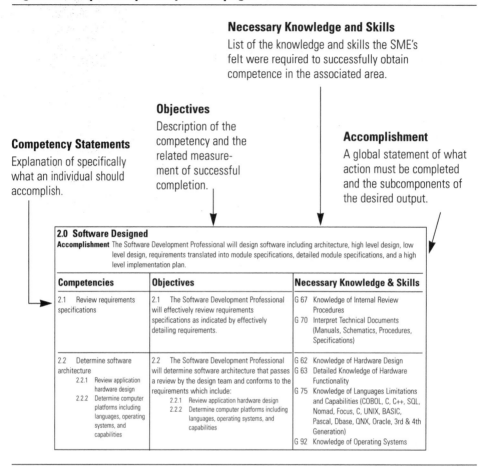

Necessary Knowledge and Skills
List of the knowledge and skills the SME's felt were required to successfully obtain competence in the associated area.

Objectives
Description of the competency and the related measurement of successful completion.

Competency Statements
Explanation of specifically what an individual should accomplish.

Accomplishment
A global statement of what action must be completed and the subcomponents of the desired output.

2.0 Software Designed

Accomplishment The Software Development Professional will design software including architecture, high level design, low level design, requirements translated into module specifications, detailed module specifications, and a high level implementation plan.

Competencies	Objectives	Necessary Knowledge & Skills
2.1 Review requirements specifications	2.1 The Software Development Professional will effectively review requirements specifications as indicated by effectively detailing requirements.	G 67 Knowledge of Internal Review Procedures G 70 Interpret Technical Documents (Manuals, Schematics, Procedures, Specifications)
2.2 Determine software architecture 2.2.1 Review application hardware design 2.2.2 Determine computer platforms including languages, operating systems, and capabilities	2.2 The Software Development Professional will determine software architecture that passes a review by the design team and conforms to the requirements which include: 2.2.1 Review application hardware design 2.2.2 Determine computer platforms including languages, operating systems, and capabilities	G 62 Knowledge of Hardware Design G 63 Detailed Knowledge of Hardware Functionality G 75 Knowledge of Languages Limitations and Capabilities (COBOL, C, C++, SQL, Nomad, Focus, C, UNIX, BASIC, Pascal, Dbase, QNX, Oracle, 3rd & 4th Generation) G 92 Knowledge of Operating Systems

developmental interventions to build the more than 300 identified knowledge and skills. A sample appears in figure 6.

3. *A management overview.* A high-level management overview course described the software engineering and systems support competency models including the benefits to be obtained, roll-out procedures, and product description.

4. *An implementation workshop.* Instructional designer EJ Romero designed, developed, and piloted an implementation workshop to train the software community in the use of the competency models. Both managers and individual contributors were to attend the one-hour hands-on workshop. After completing the workshop, participants would be able to fully utilize the competency models and resource index.

Figure 6. Sample resource index page.

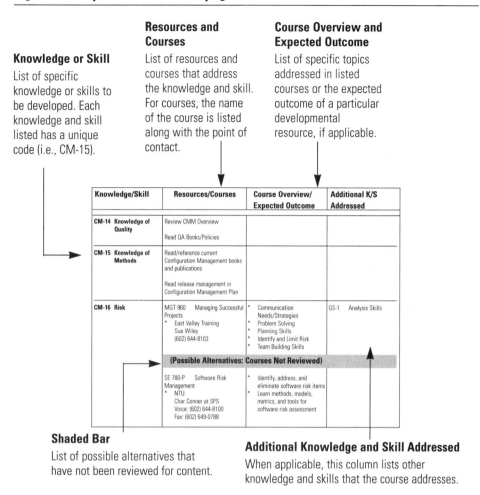

Knowledge or Skill
List of specific knowledge or skills to be developed. Each knowledge and skill listed has a unique code (i.e., CM-15).

Resources and Courses
List of resources and courses that address the knowledge and skill. For courses, the name of the course is listed along with the point of contact.

Course Overview and Expected Outcome
List of specific topics addressed in listed courses or the expected outcome of a particular developmental resource, if applicable.

Knowledge/Skill	Resources/Courses	Course Overview/ Expected Outcome	Additional K/S Addressed
CM-14 Knowledge of Quality	Review CMM Overview Read QA Books/Policies		
CM-15 Knowledge of Methods	Read/reference current Configuration Management books and publications Read release management in Configuration Management Plan		

CM-16 Risk	MGT 960 Managing Successful Projects
	* East Valley Training
	   Sue Wiley
	   (602) 644-8103
		* Communication Needs/Strategies
		* Problem Solving
		* Planning Skills
		* Identify and Limit Risk
		* Team Building Skills
			GS-1 Analysis Skills

	(Possible Alternatives: Courses Not Reviewed)		

	SE 780-P Software Risk Management
	* NTU
	   Char Conner at SPS
	   Voice: (602) 644-8100
	   Fax: (602) 649-0788
		* Identify, address, and eliminate software risk items
		* Learn methods, models, metrics, and tools for software risk assessment	

Shaded Bar
List of possible alternatives that have not been reviewed for content.

Additional Knowledge and Skill Addressed
When applicable, this column lists other knowledge and skills that the course addresses.

Rollout

To inform others of the products produced, Marilyn Kerr and David Thornewill von Essen gave informational presentations to the LATG Group level staff along and published articles in employee newsletters. They publicized the project with a major presentation during Motorola's annual total customer satisfaction project competition event.

The Software Education Council timed the implementation of this tool to coincide with the annual training planning process. The software quality assurance professionals were trained to deliver workshops for their division software professionals and their management, ensuring a timely, successful rollout of the tool to the customer base. The council identified software quality assurance engineers to deliver all workshops for their divisions, thus providing a focal point to address any questions or concerns about the tool.

All implementation workshops were complete by the end of the calendar year. This ensured that managers and employees began the next annual development process with appropriate software process training schedules.

Outcomes and Evaluation

A wide variety of benefits accrued within the organization as a result of the performance intervention. First, the desired SEI level was achieved in the time frame required. Second, an important series of training and development tools were distributed to the organization and immediately put to use to improve the quality of preparation of software specialists. Third, several other functions were able to use the outputs generated to provide additional impact within the organization, including:

1. *Individual contributor developmental tool.* Managers could reference this tool to assist them in developing their employees through the individual development planning (IDP) process and for developing their departments as requirements changed.

2. *Career planning tool.* Individual contributors used the tools for career planning purposes. They now understood clearly what requirements were necessary to achieve good performance in a variety of software functions, and they were able to develop themselves for career growth and transition into other functions.

3. *Front-end analysis tool and course development guide.* Instructional designers and training departments used these models to identify required training and areas for future course development. Training administrators used the guides as a basis for forecasting training needs.

4. *Support for performance management and a major human resources initiative designed to promote dialogue by employees and their managers.* The tools served as guides for expected performance among software professionals, supported career planning and training, and formed the basis for manager and employee dialogues.

5. *Improved software development process.* The tools supported improved quality for software products and faster development time by documenting processes and the skills required to execute them and by providing support for achieving those skills.

6. *More accurate compensation and job classifications for software engineers and system support professionals.* Compensation analysts were able

to adapt job functional data to revise job descriptions and promotional matrices.

7. *Quicker and more accurate access by the training community to course offerings and schedules.* With a current course listing at hand, training specialists were able to make rapid and informed decisions for course offerings and referrals.

The models were reviewed annually to maintain their accuracy and revised to include new courses and development options. Users had the opportunity to provide feedback on the competency resources listed, including courses.

Evaluation

Evaluation efforts included Level 1 questionnaires for the workshop, which indicated attendees' high satisfaction and acceptance. At Level 2, through exercises in the workshop, participants also indicated high satisfaction. Level 3 evaluations of use on the job were indirectly measured by course registration and achievement of the required SEI levels.

Reuse

The software engineering and system support competency models were generic and therefore easily adapted for reuse. They were widely distributed throughout Motorola. To adapt these models accurately to the needs of other groups, the following process was documented:

1. *Validate the models.* Identification of subject matter experts to validate the model content and accuracy with respect to the organization's work environment. This process increased the acceptance and use of the models within the organization. The subject matter experts had to be well recognized and respected within the organization in order for the models to carry the proper weight.

2. *Customize the resource index.* Many of the listed training resources were local vendors and thus had to be updated to reflect the group's geographic location.

3. *Coordinate with the human resources department.* The competency models could be used in support of several initiatives and standard processes in existence, including compensation, individual development plans, career planning, and performance management.

Recommendations

Competency-based performance improvement projects must be viewed as continuous improvement enterprises and require constant support. To adequately implement and maintain these programs, an active council consisting of strong business representation, dedicated instructional design and organizational effectiveness support, and energetic human resources involvement is absolutely required.

The LATG Software Education Council remained in existence to address additional needs of the software population for over a year after completion of the project. Additional key functional areas were identified as software project team leaders and software midlevel managers.

Work in support of these areas was completed one year after the initial effort and substantially contributed to its success by ensuring that managers and team leaders were knowledgeable of the requirements and developmental resources available.

Further development under the direction of Fred Berneche III and other members of the Software Council resulted in the creation of Web pages with the full software curricula and training road maps that managers and employees throughout the sector could access. Adaptation to Motorola's intranet made rapid revision possible and eliminated the need for costly paper copies.

This project, and others like it in the Semiconductor Products Sector, illustrate the need for continued involvement and close cooperation among business managers, technical experts, human resources, and skilled instructional design and development specialists. The involvement and support of a strong and innovative compensation manager is an absolute requirement for this type of project, and committed employee relations specialists frequently make or break these projects in terms of successful implementation within an organization.

Substantial work remains as new job descriptions for software professionals are developed, promotional matrices are identified, and performance management tools are introduced to managers.

Questions for Discussion

1. In a large corporation like Motorola, how might this program be leveraged for maximum cost efficiency to other divisions and sectors in their implementation of Software Engineering Institute (SEI) evaluation and adaptation? What analysis and content adjustments would be necessary to ensure appropriate transfer?

2. What cultural factors threatened the adoption of SEI standards and training for this sector? What are the probable outcomes if those factors are not addressed? Describe possible strategies for addressing these factors.

3. Discuss the most cost-efficient methods for identifying, selecting, and developing training programs, given the nature of the analysis.

4. What modern media and training delivery methods are most appropriate for diffusion of the training requirements information? How might subsequent training most effectively be delivered to the target population described in this case? In general terms, what are the cost implications and trade-offs?

5. Discuss the leadership pattern of this project. How might ISD professionals most effectively work with the technical experts assigned to lead the project? What are some alternative methods of project management?

6. Identify the implications of competency evaluation for engineers and probable ramifications for the organization. Describe a strategy for successful implementation of competency-based curriculum in this case.

The Authors

Marilyn Kerr is a training manager for Motorola's Semiconductor Products Sector in Austin, Texas. She received a B.S. in applied statistics in 1986 from Utah State University and an M.Ed. in instructional technology in 1992 from the University of Texas—Austin. Before joining Motorola, Kerr was a statistical consultant for Price Waterhouse, where she assisted U.S. government agencies in conducting cost-benefit analyses. She also worked as the continuous improvement facilitator and semiconductor wafer fab statistician for AMD/Sony Semiconductor, San Antonio, Texas, where she was responsible for statistical analysis, training, and team development activities. Kerr can be contacted at Motorola Semiconductor, 9703 Blue Hill Drive, Austin, TX 78736.

Jeremie Hill Grey is a former training manager for high-technology companies, including Intel, Singer Aerospace, and Motorola Semiconductor. At the time of this project, she was the LATG/East Valley training and development manager. Grey received her doctorate in educational media from the University of Arizona and has 20 years of professional experience in training and development for business and industry, including curriculum design and development (especially competency-based curriculum), instructional design and development, training administration, and documentation and publications. She is now a senior consultant for the Learning Consortium in Mesa, Arizona.

Notes

The authors wish to acknowledge Glen Cooper and David Thornewill von Essen for their assistance during the project and with this article.

Glen Cooper is the manager of software process and quality for Motorola's Transportation Semiconductor Group of the Semiconductor Products Sector. Prior to this position, he was manager of software initiatives for LATG. In these roles, he has responsibilities for group-wide software process and quality.

David Thornewill von Essen joined Motorola Semiconductor Products Sector in 1987, transferring to Phoenix in 1991. Essen is currently a program manager in the SPS Information Gateway, addressing the areas of e-commerce and multimedia communications.

References

Aron, Robert. (1992). *Motorola University Competency-Based Curriculum Team.* Summary Report and Presentation.

Dubois, D.D. (1993). *Competency-Based Performance Improvement.* Amherst, MA: HRD Press.

Dubois, D.D., editor. (1998). *The Competency Case Book.* Amherst, MA: HRD Press.

Rummler, G.A., & A.P. Brache. (1990). *Improving Performance: How to Manage the White Space on the Organization Chart.* San Francisco: Jossey-Bass.

Improving Roll Changeover Performance in a Manufacturing Organization

Peabody Processing Incorporated

Stephen B. King

This case documents the efforts of Peabody Processing, a steel-processing company, to improve organizational effectiveness through the application of human performance improvement (HPI). The HPI project focuses on a critical resource that happens to be the bottleneck in the plant. This resource becomes the center of the performance improvement efforts to reduce the changeover times on this machine. Background information is presented to establish the context within which the project occurs. The case then documents the approach of the human performance specialist and other key personnel and the results they achieved.

The framework for the approach is the human performance improvement process model described in ASTD Models for Human Performance Improvement *(Rothwell, 1996). First, there is a thorough analysis to define and describe what is happening and why with respect to machine changeovers. Next, several nontraining interventions are selected because of the impact they will have on changeover performance. Then these interventions are implemented through the change management process. Finally, the results are identified in the evaluation phase. In addition to describing the process, keys to success and lessons learned are included.*

Background

A multitude of performance problems, as well as opportunities, face manufacturing organizations of all sizes, in all industries. One of the primary goals of firms is to become more competitive through

This case was prepared to serve as a basis for discussion rather than to illustrate either effective or ineffective administrative and management practices.

faster response to customer needs. To achieve this end, companies strive to reduce inventory levels, decrease operating expenses, and increase throughput (Umble & Srikanth, 1990). Organizations struggle to differentiate themselves by providing superior quality, flexibility, dependability, or low price (Hayes & Wheelwright, 1984). All of this must take place in the face of intense global competition, rapid technological advances, changing consumer preferences, and a myriad of other internal and external forces.

Organizational Profile

Peabody Processing Incorporated is a steel-processing company located in the eastern United States. Peabody purchases raw material—coils of steel—from large steel producers. Peabody then processes the steel by rolling it to gauge (thickness), slitting it to width, and ensuring the proper chemical and mechanical specifications that the customer requires. Peabody is a unionized facility with approximately 280 employees. Sales in 1994 were about $200 million.

In 1995 the company embarked on a major change in its strategic direction. Top management elected to pursue a new, higher-profit-margin market, which was considered to be essentially wide open with only one major competitor. This shift meant a completely new product line that consisted of high-margin, specialty products versus the traditional low-margin, commodity products. The company had produced the low-margin products in large quantities, whereas the new, high-margin products would be low-volume items. One pressing issue was the need to facilitate the move to shorter production runs so that the manufacturing plant could adapt to customer requirements very rapidly. Traditionally, most machines in the Peabody plant would run product "A" for a long period of time, sometimes several shifts, before changing over to run product "B." With the new strategy, there would be a need to switch from "A" to "B" to "Z" in a matter of hours in some situations. For this reason, management determined that machine changeover time was critical to the organization's future success.

Critical Resource

One of the key machines in the Peabody plant is the Temper Mill. The machine is used to lightly roll a coil of steel in order to strengthen, or temper, it after being heat treated. The Temper Mill was a critical resource because it was a "bottleneck" in the plant. A bottleneck is a resource that is unable to produce quickly enough to keep pace with demand. For this reason, it ran three shifts per day and six or seven days per week. The Temper Mill uses chrome-plated rolls that determine the surface finish that is transferred to the coil of steel. When rolls become marked, or when a different product is scheduled, they must be changed.

Key Players

Thomas Williams is the manager responsible for the Temper Mill. Dave Johnson, Janice Watson, and Henry Ames are the three primary Temper Mill operators for each of the three shifts. Each operator has a crew of three that assists with the operation of the mill. Jay Forest is the performance improvement specialist. Gary Sullivan is the maintenance supervisor for the Peabody facility. Julio Franco is a lead mechanic who reports to Sullivan. The plant manager for the operation is George Baker.

Getting Started

Once Jay Forest had identified the bottleneck resource, it was time to get to work. The conceptual framework from which Forest planned to operate is similar to the HPI process that Rothwell (1996) described. This process involves performance analysis, cause analysis, intervention selection, implementation, change management, and evaluation. Rothwell also identified four roles associated with performance improvement: analyst, intervention specialist, change manager, and evaluator. Using this model, Forest requested a meeting with Williams, the manager of the Temper Mill. In this initial meeting Forest outlined a possible approach he believed could be used to achieve changeover performance improvement. He explained that it was important to analyze the current situation before taking any action. Williams, a "Type A" personality who liked to make things happen quickly, balked at this notion. He explained that, in his mind, doing extensive time studies and countless hours of data analysis were a waste of valuable time. Every minute spent "studying the problem" was time away from "getting to the solution." Forest assured Williams that he had no intention of getting into "analysis paralysis" and that he had been down that road and did not like the view either. Forest stood his ground and insisted that some preliminary analysis be conducted. He further explained that by doing so, the company would have a better understanding of the problem and its causes and they would have a mechanism in place by which to measure progress. Eventually, Williams became convinced and agreed to begin with an analysis of the changeover process.

Forest then quickly reviewed the other phases that would follow analysis. He explained to Williams that once the analysis was completed, the next step was to choose the appropriate intervention to improve the situation. Forest alerted Williams to the fact that a large number of solutions might be possible, but the key is to choose the right one or ones. He used the metaphor of a physician to summarize the essence of the HPI steps of analysis and intervention selection. Forest explained that a doctor never approaches a patient and immediately writes up a prescription. A competent physician always takes time to ask questions of the patient and diagnose the problem. Forest explained that this is equivalent to the analysis phase. Then, once a patient has been accurately diagnosed, the physician would prescribe the appropriate intervention. Similar to the physician, after analyzing the Temper Mill situation, the team could prescribe one or more appropriate solutions.

The next phase that Forest described was implementation. He told Williams that this would be the fun part because this is where the intervention would be implemented through change management. Williams acknowledged that he was anxious for implementation but did not want to wait too long to get there.

Finally, Forest explained to Williams that once the interventions were implemented it was critical to measure success. He labeled this the "evaluation phase." A variety of questions that often remain unanswered will be addressed in the evaluation phase. Did we see an improvement in performance? How much improvement was seen? What is the value of the improvement? What should we change, discontinue, or revisit? What lessons did we learn? Williams agreed that most improvement efforts at Peabody were poorly evaluated if they were evaluated at all. The plant had a history of moving from project to project with no formal evaluation of the impact.

Once Forest and Williams were in agreement on the general game plan, a meeting was called with all of the operators and helpers on the Temper Mill. Before this meeting, Forest asked Williams to lead the discussion with the group to explain the need for the project and the strategy that would be taken. Williams agreed and asked Forest to participate as well. During the meeting it quickly became obvious that Johnson, the senior operator and union official with 27 years of experience, was the skeptic. Johnson assumed that reducing the roll changeover times equated to reducing the workforce. To offset Johnson's skepticism, much of the meeting was dedicated to explaining the business imperative of the improvement efforts. Watson, a

younger, but outspoken operator, and two of the helpers bought into the idea more readily, especially when the discussion focused on
foreign competition and long-term job security and growth. These
employees began to express their understanding of the effort to Johnson and eventually his explicit resistance began to wane.

Analysis
Review of Production Reports

The first step in the effort to analyze the current roll-change situation was to examine the production reports that the Temper Mill
operators completed every shift. These reports contained information
such as coil run time, length of machine downtime, reason for downtime, operator notes, and changeover time. Surprisingly, although
changeover time was recorded on the production reports, it was rarely
used beyond that. Forest gathered the last three months' reports, dust-
ed off his calculator, and determined that rolls were changed on the
Temper Mill approximately two times per day, or .67 times per shift.
He also determined that the average time for each changeover was
approximately 1.5 hours.

Forest decided that it was important to go a step beyond simply
documenting the average time for a changeover. The important question was, How much would performance improvement be worth? To
obtain financial information, Forest scheduled a meeting with the plant
manager, George Baker. Forest was pleased that Baker was more than
willing to share all of the financial data he possessed. Forest learned
that a financial measure existed that essentially said, given demand
from customers, each hour the Temper Mill was in operation, it was
worth approximately $1,200. Baker explained to Forest that this was
a "rough" approximation based on the previous year's product mix,
profit margins, operating expenses, and several other financial metrics. Baker explained that in terms of roll changes, it essentially "cost"
Peabody $1,200 for every hour the mill was idle. Another point that
Baker made was that with the move to a higher margin product mix
in the future, the figure would increase substantially. Using this measure, Forest made the calculations shown below:

On average there are two changeovers per day. Each changeover
takes 1.5 hours, so a total of 2 x 1.5 = 3 hours per day is spent in changeovers.
The Temper Mill currently runs 26 days per month. This means that
roughly 3 x 26 = 78 hours per month are spent in changeovers. Because the Temper Mill cost is $1,200 per hour, the monthly cost in
idle time due to changeovers is 78 x $1,200 = $93,600. If this is pro-

jected to an annual figure, the time spent in Temper Mill changeovers becomes $93,600 x 12 months per year = $1,123,200.

Documenting the Changeover Steps

The next step in the analysis phase was to document the crews' steps during a roll changeover. To accomplish this, all operators and helpers were assembled in a conference room. Forest and Williams led the group in a modified brainstorming session to identify each of the steps in the process. During the brainstorming, Ames, a Temper Mill operator, suggested that a videotape be taken during a changeover so that all steps could be captured more completely. Johnson, the senior operator, immediately resisted this suggestion because he felt it could be used against the crew in the future. Williams, the Temper Mill manager, made a convincing argument to Johnson that videotaping was an easy way to ensure that all tasks were considered. He also guaranteed that a video would not be used to incriminate anyone.

Two days later a changeover being performed by Watson, the second shift operator, was captured using a video camera. Forest and Williams then viewed it to document all of the steps that were missed during the brainstorming session. A total of 137 steps were identified and documented. A partial list of the steps in the changeover and the approximate time for each is shown in table 1.

In addition to simply listing the steps in the process, Forest felt it would be powerful to present a graphical representation of the roll

Table 1. Partial list of Temper Mill changeover steps.

Step #	Description of Activity	Time
25	Obtain wrench from tool box.	150 seconds
26	Shut off air pressure.	15 seconds
27	Walk to main panel.	10 seconds
28	Loosen four bolts.	45 seconds
29	Remove main cover plate.	25 seconds
30	Obtain oil soaked rags from basket.	90 seconds
31	Test pressure.	25 seconds
32	Walk to pump and turn "on."	45 seconds
33	Wait for oil transfer process.	280 seconds

changeover. To accomplish this he extracted a graphic of the Temper Mill from a blueprint and drew lines representing the physical movement that took place as each of the 137 steps was carried out. This graphic is displayed in figure 1.

Once the production report and changeover steps were collected, they were presented to the Temper Mill crew during the next meet-

Figure 1. Graphical Representation of a Temper Mill Roll Changeover.

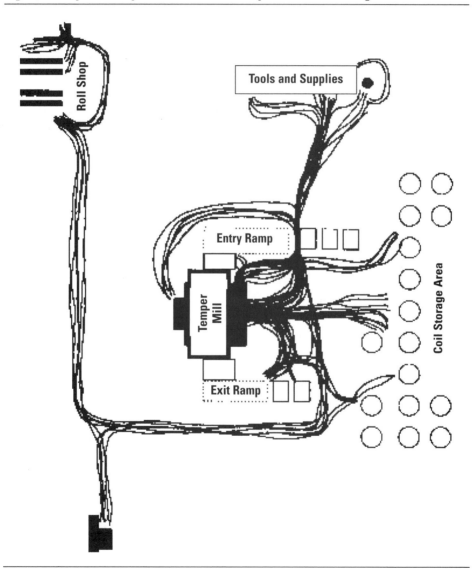

ing. The graphic showing the Temper Mill changeover (figure 1) left the greatest impression on the group. Several operators and helpers, including senior operator Johnson, were shocked that there was so much movement involved. Watson quipped, "No wonder I don't feel like exercising after work. I must walk three miles during the changeover alone."

Identifying Internal and External Steps

Forest asked the group if after viewing the steps currently involved in a changeover, they thought that there were any ways it could be improved. Several people commented that there was a large amount of time spent waiting and walking to get things. These comments provided Forest with a perfect introduction to the concepts of internal and external changeover activities. He explained that internal activities are those that could only be performed when the Temper Mill was not running. Removing rolls from the machine is an example of an internal activity because it could not be done while the machine is running. External activities are those that could be performed while the Temper Mill was still in operation (Shingo, 1985). For example, gathering the tools that would be needed during the changeover is an external activity. Forest concluded by saying that large reductions in changeover times could probably be achieved by performing external activities while the machine was running before the changeover, instead of when it was idle.

Intervention Selection

After the analysis comes the selection of the appropriate intervention or interventions to improve on the current situation. The company employed four primary interventions.

Intervention One: Job Redesign

During the same meeting, Forest engaged the group in a discussion to identify which of the 137 steps in the Temper Mill changeover were internal and which were external activities. He also asked the crew to identify improvements and changes that could be made to the existing process to reduce the changeover time.

After studying the data and discussing the steps, it was determined that approximately 35 percent of the tasks that were currently performed during a roll change were actually external activities. The group concluded that simply redesigning the way the changeover was carried out—performing external activities while the machine was still running—should result in significant improvement.

The group also identified many tasks that could be modified or changed so they would be done more efficiently. For example, the operators had to walk to the back of the machine twice during a changeover, once to turn a switch to "off" and later turn it "on." The group determined that if this button were moved to the main control panel, they could save a total of about two minutes and 30 seconds during each changeover. Even though using this button was an internal activity because it could not take place during Temper Mill operation, the speed by which it was performed could be greatly improved upon.

Intervention Two: Tooling and Equipment Modification

Another intervention that the group considered at the same meeting was the use of different or modified tooling and equipment to make the changeover tasks more efficient. For example, Johnson, the senior operator, suggested that quick disconnect fittings on hoses could be installed to replace the currently used fittings that had to be manually screwed on. Quick disconnect hoses would enable operators to remove the hoses quickly and easily without the use of a wrench.

During another meeting, one of the helpers suggested purchasing an air-driven drill to use when removing and installing bolts from an oil plate. Currently, four bolts were manually loosened and later tightened using a bar with a drill. The helper believed that using an air drill would speed up this process significantly and make it safer as well. When this suggestion was presented, Williams picked up the phone and paged Sullivan, the plant maintenance supervisor. Seconds later Sullivan called and Williams briefly explained the idea and informed Sullivan that he would like to see someone from the maintenance department at the meeting. Within minutes Julio Franco, one of the lead mechanics, arrived, and the group explained the idea of using an air drill. After hearing the idea, Franco complimented the group and suggested that there might be an even less expensive way to accomplish this. Franco said that "half-turn" bolts could be installed. Franco explained that bolts could be altered by putting slots along the length of the bolt. Instead of screwing the bolt into the hole, which frequently requires many turns, the bolt was slid in and then only turned 180 degrees to secure it. The group liked Franco's idea even though it still required manual removal of the bolts. They decided that the bolts were not large enough to warrant an air drill.

Intervention Three: Establish Performance Goals and Standards

As Forest reviewed the production records from the previous three months, he noticed that there seemed to be a large variation in the changeover times. He calculated that the average time for a changeover was 90 minutes, but the lowest time he saw was 70 seconds and the highest time was 255 minutes. Forest had a discussion with Williams about this variation and asked if any roll change standards existed. Forest was somewhat surprised to learn that there were not only no changeover standards, but also no production standards that were strictly adhered to.

Forest explained the benefits and usefulness of goals and standards, pointing out that the lack of standards could be part of the reason for such inconsistency in changeover times. Williams agreed, and in a team meeting he made the case for establishing changeover standards. He wanted to avoid imposing standards in order to get buy-in from the group. To do this, he and Forest led the group in a discussion about the benefits of goals and standards. In addition to the organizational benefits that Williams suggested, the group mentioned many other benefits. For example, Ames commented that achievement of the goal or standard would not only cause them to stretch, it would provide a sense of pride and satisfaction.

Williams asked the group what they felt comfortable with, knowing that the average changeover time was 90 minutes. After some debate and discussion, the group decided that 75 minutes for a changeover within two months was a good place to start, and it could be revisited later. Forest presented the approximation of the cost savings of a 15-minute reduction in changeover time over one year. When Johnson, the senior operator, heard that about $187,200 could be saved annually, he began to grow irate and wanted to know who would pocket the savings. The other operators began to question this as well. Williams explained that he wished some of it could go to everyone directly, but unfortunately there was no incentive system in place to reward improvements. However, he related his confidence that such savings would allow the company to reinvest in the operation and provide job security in the long run.

Intervention Four: Establish Feedback System

In addition to setting performance goals and standards, Forest explained the importance of feedback as a means of performance improvement. Williams was somewhat surprised to hear about the impact of feedback as well as the benefits that employees, managers, and the organization could gain by using a variety of feedback mechanisms (Stoneman, Bancroft, & Halling, 1995). When properly delivered, feedback helps employees to understand where they are compared to where they should be in terms of performance. It is useful for providing a clear picture so that everyone is reading from the same page. Another meeting took place with all of the Temper Mill personnel to discuss feedback.

One team member suggested that because changeover standards had been established, a bulletin board could be posted to monitor progress. The operators could be responsible for posting their changeover times on the board. In this way, instant feedback would be provided regarding individual and group performance (Greif, 1991). Several people brought up the point that some operators might be tempted to cheat or would not buy in to the idea. Williams explained how he saw it working by stating that the bulletin board would be a way to track and celebrate performance improvement and would not be used for punishment. He also explained that it could also serve as a communication tool because when problems were encountered they would become visible immediately. In essence, the problems highlighted on the board could initiate team meetings to discuss and learn from the problems and to solve them. Everyone agreed that this would be very helpful because often problems were left unaddressed.

Implementation and Change Management

It is interesting to note that the performance improvement cycle with the Temper Mill occurred in a dynamic fashion. In other words, it did not progress linearly from analysis to intervention selection to implementation to evaluation. For example, once the group decided that performance goals and standards would be useful, the goal of 75 minutes per changeover was established and implemented almost immediately. Further, once the team agreed on the type of board and the layout, Williams placed an order the following day. Within four days team members were using it.

In the area of performing external changeover activities while the machine was running, certain changes could be implemented quickly. For example, traditionally once the machine stopped running, employees would locate the tools and bring them to the machine. After identifying this potential improvement area, the group revised the activity so that one of the employees got the tools before the machine shut down. By performing this task while the Temper Mill was in operation, the tools would be ready for use immediately. There were many other external activities that employees began to perform during machine operation. Some of these changes were implemented rapidly, but others required more time and coordination especially when more than one person or someone from outside the Temper Mill was involved. Williams and Forest held meetings with the crew and brought others in as necessary. In these meetings, they discussed ideas and formed action and implementation plans that they put into motion.

In addition to the job redesign efforts, many incremental improvements were instituted that made the changeover process more efficient and easier. Team members made some of the changes themselves. Others required help from outside departments, especially maintenance. Williams and Forest developed a strong relationship with Sullivan, the maintenance supervisor, because they worked closely to implement many changes. For example, before the change effort, the operators had to walk behind the machine to press a button. To eliminate this wasted time and effort, maintenance rewired the button and located it on the main control panel, within reach of the operator. Also, prior to the performance improvement effort, the new set of rolls that were inserted into the mill were stored in the roll grinding area, which was about 500 feet from the mill. To improve upon this situation, maintenance moved a storage rack to within 15 feet of the machine. When the changeover began, the rolls only had to be moved a fraction of the distance.

Evaluation

Like the implementation and change management phase, the evaluation phase occurred on a continuous basis, not linearly. In other words, Forest did not wait until everything was implemented to evaluate the results. Because standards and feedback vehicles were in place, he simply monitored progress continuously. It was easy to determine whether or not changes and improvements that were being introduced had an impact. For example, it was easy to see that before a change was implemented it took 50 seconds to perform a task, whereas it only took 20 seconds after modification of the procedure. Forest and Williams held ongoing meetings and brief communication sessions with operators at the machine to update them on changes and the impact of these changes. As performance improvement was realized, a sense of excitement was generated among the team, as well as throughout the organization.

The changeover times during the first six months of the project appear in figure 2. After six months, the group had achieved a reduction in changeover time of 50 percent. This average improvement of 45 minutes translates into savings of $22,880. This figure does not include the number of hours that were now available to run additional products.

Figure 2. Reduction in Temper Mill changeover time from May through November.

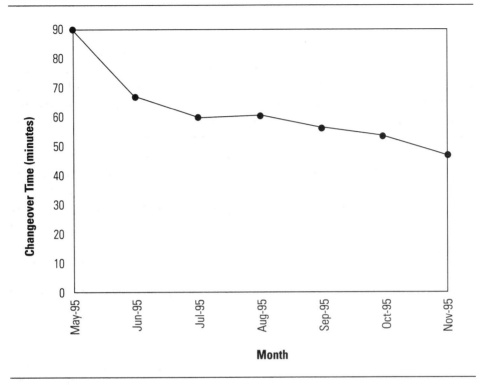

Celebrating the Results

Baker, the plant manager, asked Forest and Williams to give a presentation on the results of the project during an upcoming quarterly meeting for all employees at Peabody. Forest and Williams decided to make it a true team effort by asking some of the Temper Mill employees to participate. During the meeting, the participants outlined the entire performance improvement process and highlighted the benefits that resulted. In addition to the cost savings and productivity improvement, many changes resulted in safer work practices. Additionally, a sense of teamwork and improved morale began to take shape within the Temper Mill crew as well as between management and employees. Williams concluded the presentation by stating that the work was both challenging and rewarding, but it was far from over. He added his hope that the lessons learned and improvements made at the Temper Mill could be transferred to other areas of Peabody Processing.

Conclusion and Lessons Learned

When Forest was asked to reflect on the Temper Mill performance improvement project, the importance of communication came to his mind as a key learning component. Forest recognized early in the process that without the support, input, and commitment of a variety of people within the organization, the results would have been difficult, if not impossible, to accomplish. In fact, Stolovitch, Keeps, and Rodrigue (1995) contend that effective communication with a variety of stakeholders is a vital skill for human performance technologists to possess. Williams, the Temper Mill manager, was one of the key players that had to be on board to ensure success of the project. Forest spent a great deal of time at the beginning communicating with Williams about the HPI process, roles to be played, and the need for his support and commitment. Like many managers, Williams wanted to make things happen quickly, and Forest found himself trying to put on the brakes to accomplish important activities, such as the initial analysis. Such struggles are consistent with research by Rossett and Czech (1995) who found that "making the case for needs assessment" was a major problem that performance improvement specialists encountered. Through persistent and clear communication, however, Forest was able to adopt a partnership with Williams that allowed them to achieve dramatic outcomes. Robinson and Robinson (1995) discuss the importance of forming a partnership in great detail.

Many models that portray the human performance improvement process are linear. Forest quickly discovered that it is quite impossible and impractical to move sequentially from step one to step two, and so on. HPI is a dynamic process that often moves rapidly and changes as it evolves. He found that there were often steps that overlapped, continued throughout the project, and were employed only as needed. For example, when the analysis phase (phase one) was still taking place, interventions were being selected (phase two), implemented (phase three), and evaluated (phase four). Forest found it necessary, yet challenging, to maintain a balance between thorough analysis and quick results. Several times Forest had to pull in the reigns on Williams because he was going after a quick fix before it was clear that the direction was appropriate.

From the beginning, improving the performance of the Temper Mill changeovers had a focus on results. Human performance improvement is bottom-line oriented because it focuses on performance-based problems and opportunities. Kirkpatrick (1994) developed a model for evaluating training programs. The Temper Mill project centered around his level four, bottom-line results. In effect, Forest did not have to worry about measuring levels one (reaction), two (learning), or three (behavior change). All of his time, energy, and focus was on improving performance results. From the outcomes that were achieved, his efforts paid off in more ways than one.

Questions for Discussion

1. Why was the Temper Mill chosen as the target of the performance improvement effort?
2. Discuss the selection process that was used in identifying this resource as the area of focus and the rationale for that choice.
3. How would you describe the approach that Forest, the performance improvement specialist, used in this HPI effort? Discuss the role that involvement of others played.
4. Discuss the importance of interaction skills and communication skills in this effort in particular and in HPI efforts in general.
5. Was the analysis work that was conducted effective? Why or why not? In your discussion, include the issue of "analysis paralysis" and the balance that must be maintained between achieving results quickly and collecting solid data about the situation.
6. This case discusses four interventions that were implemented. Can you think of other interventions that could be used?
7. What could Forest have done differently to be more effective in his efforts?

The Author

Stephen B. King is a Ph.D. candidate in Workforce Education and Development at The Pennsylvania State University. He expects to graduate in December 1998. He currently works as an independent organizational performance consultant. His research focuses on the competencies associated with the role of the HPI analyst. Prior to graduate school, King held a variety of positions in a Fortune 500 manufacturing organization. He has presented at the International Society for Performance Improvement and the American Society for Training & Development's international conferences and has several publications related to training and performance improvement. He holds a B.S. in business administration and an M.A. in adult education from the Ohio State University. He can be contacted at the following address: 927-5 West Whitehall Road, State College, PA 16801.

References

Greif, M. (1991). *The Visual Factory: Building Participation Through Shared Information*. Cambridge, MA: Productivity Press.

Hayes, R.H., and S.C. Wheelwright. (1984). *Restoring Our Competitive Edge: Competing Through Manufacturing*. New York: John Wiley.

Kirkpatrick, D.L. (1994). *Evaluating Training Programs: The Four Levels*. Emeryville, CA: Berrett-Koehler.

Robinson, D.G., and J.C. Robinson. (1995). *Performance Consulting: Moving Beyond Training*. San Francisco: Berrett-Koehler.

Rossett, A., and C. Czech. (1995). "They Really Wanna, But. . . The Aftermath of Professional Preparation in Performance Technology." *Performance Improvement Quarterly, 8*(4), 115-132.

Rothwell, W.J. (1996). *The ASTD Models For Human Performance Improvement: Roles, Competencies, and Outputs*. Alexandria, VA: ASTD.

Shingo, S. (1985). *A Revolution in Manufacturing: The SMED System*. Cambridge, MA: Productivity Press.

Stolovitch, H.D., E.J. Keeps, and D. Rodrigue. (1995). "Skill Sets for the Human Performance Technologist." *Performance Improvement Quarterly, 8*(2), 40-67.

Stoneman, K., E. Bancroft, and C. Halling. (1995). "Upward Feedback for Organizational Change." *Performance and Instruction, 34*(7), 12-17.

Umble, M.M., and M.L. Srikanth. (1990). *Synchronous Manufacturing: Principles for World-Class Manufacturing*. Cincinnati: South-Western.

Responding to Competitive Pressures With Integrated HR Systems

Southern California Gas Company

Calvin C. Hoffman and John M. Stormes

Southern California Gas Company (SoCalGas) developed integrated human resources systems to respond to actual and anticipated changes in the competitive marketplace for energy and energy distribution services. These new systems are the result of joint efforts of many company groups including employee development, business solutions, labor relations, local distribution services, and transmission and storage. Numerous changes—regulatory, competitive, social, and technological—are having an impact on this and many other companies. SoCalGas has responded by decreasing costs, restructuring to focus on its core business, and drastically redesigning the work of its union-represented operations workforce. Changes in job design had a significant impact on training, selection, compensation, and job placement systems, leading to ongoing rethinking and experimentation to refine their processes. The integrated systems approach emerging from this work is expected to position the company so as to face future challenges, like unbundling of services and aggressive competition, with considerably more confidence than could have been mustered when these potential threats emerged some 10 years ago.

Background
Pre-1991

Training and other human resources systems at SoCalGas have not always been unified, and training itself has moved through several different incarnations. Until about 1991, the training function was divided among several departments. Management training was

This case was prepared to serve as a basis for discussion rather than to illustrate either effective or ineffective administrative and management practices.

part of human resources (HR), although it was geographically located apart from the rest of HR. In contrast, the technical training units, which trained nonmanagement-represented employees, were part of operations staff groups. There was relatively little interaction among the different training groups, or between them and the rest of HR. It was not uncommon for them to work on projects, which overlapped or were even at cross-purposes with one another.

1991 to 1995

During these years, the company went through a series of reorganization efforts with the goals of eliminating low-value activities, reducing head count, and redesigning the organizational structure so as to better serve customers at lower cost. The technical and management training organizations were centralized under one mid-level manager, resulting in the creation of an organizational development (OD) group. During this time, the training and development department made significant efforts to strengthen the competence of the training staff. Its selection of instructors was more rigorous through the use of role plays and simulations, and the department encouraged ongoing development of training skills.

A significant project undertaken to provide a long-term road map for corporate training called for increased use of aptitude-based selection systems, increased rigor in technical training, including pass-fail testing, and increased competence of instructors. By the end of this period, all training and OD reported to one director, and an internally developed and delivered instructor certification program was in operation.

1995 to 1998

The company adopted its current business unit organizational form in mid-1995, during a corporate restructuring in which training was decentralized. Technical training was carved into four sections, each reporting to a team leader; whereas management training, instructional design, organizational consulting, and personnel assessment functions were placed under one middle-level manager in a support unit comprised of other HR service functions as well. Even though the training function was "dismantled" during restructuring, training as a corporate identity gained significant influence because of the high level of collaboration and values that the five training units shared both before and after restructuring.

Industry Profile

Natural gas transmission and distribution is a major industry in the United States. Natural gas is classified as a fossil fuel because it is generally released from oil fields and its principal component is methane, the simplest hydrocarbon (one carbon atom combined with four hydrogen atoms). Natural gas has been regulated throughout its history both as a natural monopoly within local distribution areas and through price control and other federal regulations applied to its production and transmission.

Most gas distribution companies are quite small with customers totaling in the thousands and employees in the hundreds or less. Several publicly owned energy utilities sell both gas and electricity, including Pacific Gas and Electric in northern California and San Diego Gas and Electric in San Diego County, California.

Energy transmission and distribution industries are undergoing deregulation at the present time, which provides a major impetus for restructuring the company into business units. At the federal level, price controls on natural gas production began to be lifted in the 1970s, and interstate transmission has been allowed to expand with little regard for the jurisdiction of state public utility commissions or existing monopolistic franchises within states. At the state level, the focus of regulation has shifted from long-term security of supply to lowest cost, so competition from spot-market resellers and out-of-state transmission companies has forced local distribution companies to rethink the ways in which they purchase gas and what level of overhead is absolutely essential for competitive and efficient operation.

Safety, service, and convenience at a low cost are still the gas distribution industry's major concerns. Therefore, thoroughly trained employees who can work on the customer's premises with a professional demeanor and perform competently are essential in order to provide the organization's competitive edge.

Organizational Profile

The Southern California Gas Company is the largest publicly owned natural gas utility in the United States, with 7,200 employees at the end of 1995. Its service area covers most of southern California south of Fresno, except for San Diego County. The company has about 4,700,000 customers, most of whom are residential and small business. The main functions of the company are the transmission and storage of natural gas, 90 percent of which comes from outside California, and the distribution of natural gas to individual customers.

In July 1995, SoCalGas was restructured into two business units regulated by the California Public Utilities Commission (CPUC): Energy Distribution Services (EDS) and Energy Transportation Services (ETS). EDS is responsible for local distribution and most marketing. ETS is responsible for the transmission and storage of natural gas for both EDS and very large customers (such as electric power and other gas utilities), to whom they deliver gas directly. Unregulated business units of the parent company, Pacific Enterprises, took ownership of any functions within SoCalGas that did not require CPUC regulation. Every business unit, whether regulated or not, is individually responsible for its own business results under this new corporate structure, which is intended to strengthen the company's competitiveness in the face of pressure to deregulate the natural gas industry and lower costs.

HRD Function Profile
Organization

The HR responsibilities are distributed among the business units and the corporation, Pacific Enterprises. Corporate HR sets overall policy, and its human resource development (HRD) functions, such as executive development and diversity, are those having corporate policy implications.

The other centralized HRD functions supporting the business units, especially EDS and ETS which make up SoCalGas, are in the personnel department within EDS Support Services. The decentralized HRD functions, essentially technical training, are located in strategic planning departments in the other business units. (Figure 1 depicts the breakdown in its illustration of training in a business unit on the left and personnel functions in support services on the right.) Management training is included with development consulting in personnel.

Current Challenges

Like many other companies, SoCalGas has dealt with a wide array of changes that have an impact on its operations. In common with other utilities, the company is operating in a changing regulatory environment. Deregulation will soon lead to performance-based rates and the unbundling of services that now appear in customers' monthly bills as a maintenance fee and a portion of the price of gas. Additionally, social and demographic and technological changes are becoming more apparent. Due to the changing demographic mix in

Figure 1. Centralized HRD functions and an example of decentralized functions in the EDS business unit.

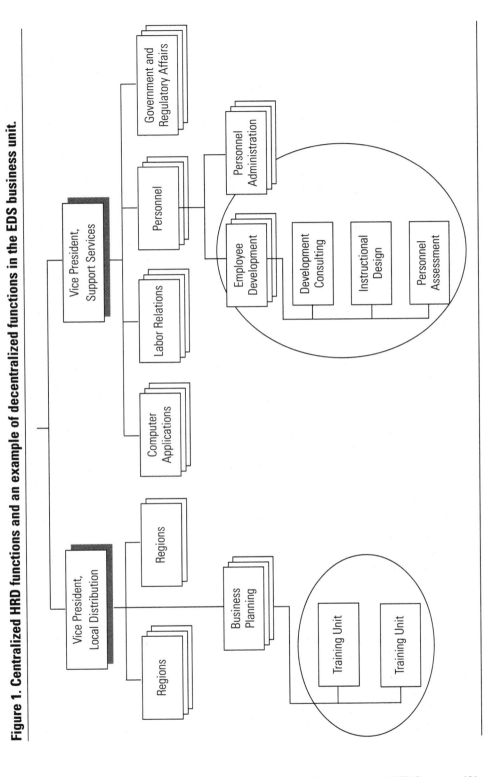

the external labor market, the company is experiencing a decrease in the average level of skills available in the candidate pool. Technological changes are apparent in the increased use of computers and other electronic equipment. Such technology often increases the average complexity of the work to be performed. The combination of increased skill requirements coupled with the decrease of available skills creates a skills gap that many organizations are struggling to overcome.

Approaches to Human Performance Improvement

This chapter argues that the best way for the HR function to provide support in the current competitive environment is for it to assume a consultative role. To succeed in that role, it must partner closely with clients, evaluating short- and long-term business needs, and building agile HR systems responsive to changing organizational needs. The HR interventions described here began in 1993, before the corporate restructuring, and are still evolving.

Consulting Model

Before the restructuring of SoCalGas in mid-1995, training was in the early stages of defining a set of shared values intended to unite its various units, despite the fact that they all reported to the same director. Historically, the technical training units had focused more on moving trainees through classes and back to the field rather than making sure they had fully achieved and demonstrated the competencies they needed. Training was typically not pass-fail, instructional design principles were rarely, if ever, incorporated into training design, and little consistent evaluation of training was conducted.

This approach started to change about the time of the restructuring. The aforementioned instructor certification and selection programs helped unite training units, providing a common vision for how training "should be." The trainer certification program included modules on needs assessment, consulting skills, instructional design, program evaluation, and adult learning principles and facilitation. Training as an organization became less of an order taker and more of a partner with client groups.

As training and development currently operates, the employee development (ED) staff functions as an internal consultant regarding instructional design, management training, assessment, personal computer (PC) training, and organizational consulting. It partners with the four technical training groups, which are closely aligned with the processes they support in the business units. ED also partners with the HR policy group in the parent company on activities such as multirater 360 feedback, training delivery, and career issues.

Cost-Reduction Efforts

The Southern California Gas Company, as an organization, has responded to competitive pressures by decreasing costs and becoming more sensitive to customer needs. In 1992, the company embarked on a series of projects known as Activity Value Analyses (AVAs) designed to reduce overhead. AVAs had the goal of reducing costs by evaluating the activities performed by a department and, then, finding ways to reduce or eliminate activities found to be of low value. Typically, each department completed AVAs, with marketing and human resources being the first to be reorganized. In late 1994 and 1995, the company restructured into business units, its current organizational design, consolidating the efficiencies achieved to focus more directly on the customer.

As a result of these and other initiatives during the last 10 years, SoCalGas has made great strides in reducing its costs and streamlining operations: the workforce decreased from 10,600 to around 7,200, the number of operating divisions dropped from 18 to eight (and, soon six), and the number of management layers dropped from seven to four or five.

In addition to cost-reduction programs and corporate restructuring, the company has moved aggressively to redesign work at the field level (job reclassification) to help it prepare for both performance-based rate-making and unbundling. The company's operations leadership recognized the need to redesign field jobs if the company were to meet customer needs and long-term productivity goals. At odds with this need was the existing collective bargaining agreement, which hampered the company's competitiveness with numerous restrictions on a range of issues, particularly in the area of workforce flexibility. What job reclassification entails and how the HR systems must be coordinated to achieve the desired performance improvement and competitive cost structure will be explained in the balance of this chapter.

Overview of Reclassification

Workforce flexibility was a key theme in the reclassification project. As field operations jobs evolved over time, they became relatively fragmented. Both the local distribution and transmission regions assigned teams to evaluate how their field work was structured and to recommend how it could be made more efficient. They found that it was often necessary to send a second or third employee to a customer's location to complete a job, reducing both customer satisfaction and efficiency. The local distribution and transmission teams independently concluded that the job classifications were too specialized and the number needed to be drastically reduced, providing a more flexible workforce in broader jobs. Before the reclassification project, employees in roughly 50 separate job classifications performed field work. When it is fully implemented, field work will be performed in about 28 classifications.

The impact of the reclassification project was extensive. Besides requiring drastic union contract changes and job redesign, it required all-new HR systems, including training, selection, compensation, and job placement systems. Client organizations owned, sponsored, and managed the overall project; it was not HR driven but, rather, HR supported and coordinated. There was a major collaboration of three groups: operations field (local distribution services, transmission, storage), related support groups (business solutions, technical training) and numerous HR groups (employee development, compensation, labor relations, personnel administration). This chapter includes an overview of how these HR systems had to change to meet this major challenge.

Description of the Effort
Issues That Triggered the Activity

JOB FAMILY PROJECTS. In 1994 the company's personnel research group conducted two projects, the Comprehensive Selection System (CSS) and Physical Ability Test (PAT), aimed at expanding the application of both cognitive and physical ability tests to a wider range of jobs. Both projects relied on existing company research regarding selection systems and an existing database on the Position Analysis Questionnaire (PAQ). The company uses the PAQ for job evaluation, but this job analysis instrument has numerous other applications.

Using existing PAQ data as a starting point, both projects applied statistical methods (cluster analysis) and review of statistical findings by company job experts (supervisors, technical training personnel) to develop job families. Cognitive ability tests and PATs were set up according to job family, allowing the company to leverage existing selection research. A second major product of these projects was the development of job-slotting procedures. The job-slotting procedures are quantitatively based and allow the company to design a new job, complete a PAQ covering its proposed content, assign it to a job family, and set up selection systems before the new job exists. The slotting procedure is extremely efficient because PAQs were already required to determine a new job's pay grade.

Although the CSS and PAT projects were completed over two years before the reclassification project began, the company could not implement them at the time for several reasons. Most of the jobs in question were union. Implementing tests on a scale this broad required major contractual changes. There was no HR infrastructure in place to support testing at this volume given that, at that time, some tests were scored by hand. Finally, many clients needed to be informed about this work. The timing was simply wrong.

A number of things happened during the intervening years that allowed the results of the CSS and PAT projects to be applied. The company restructured into business units, there was increased competition and pressure to reduce costs, there was a greater acceptance of testing both in training and in selection, and the technical training organization (a major client) asked for more selection testing. Client organizations were also in a position to redesign their represented jobs, in preparation for negotiating a new contract, which would have been too difficult to attempt between union contracts.

COURSE MODULARIZATION. A project completed by instructional design and technical training groups during 1993-1994 piloted the steps needed to modularize training while redesigning the course for field service representatives (FSRs). Instructional design staff worked with instructors and represented employees in redesigning these courses into modules. The modular training materials allowed more content to be provided more effectively to employees in the same amount of time. Additionally, materials like pass-fail tests and checklists helped instructors provide better feedback and instruction to employees.

Shortly after completion of the modularization pilot, the company needed to repackage FSR training to support a flexible workforce initiative. Using the new modular training materials, the designers completed all revisions in about two weeks, rather than the several months previously required for changes of this magnitude, a significant increase in efficiency.

Description of the Initiative

The HR initiative was to support the reclassification of field jobs, from analysis and design of jobs through selection, training, and placement utilizing a consultative approach. The anticipated outcome was to achieve the cost-reduction and performance improvement goals of field management as quickly and effectively as possible without disrupting management-union relations or creating undue hardship on the routine operations of the company.

Targeted Goals and Population

All HR activities in this initiative were directed at upgrading the skills of approximately 2,500 experienced field workers, all union members, to reach the goal of a more flexible workforce within about three years.

The typical field worker has 10 to 20 years of experience with SoCalGas. Almost all have a high school education, although many have inadequate reading and math skills. Both men and women hold field jobs, although many positions are predominately held by men.

Key Issues and Events
Job Redesign

The earlier work with job families supporting broader use of testing also helped prompt thinking on ways to combine jobs. Job design teams considered a range of factors in developing their proposed jobs, including customers' needs, workforce flexibility, workforce diversity, and cognitive and physical ability requirements. The teams redesigned roughly 50 existing jobs into about 28 jobs. In most cases, the new jobs were created by combining pieces of two to four jobs. A few new jobs were created by splitting existing jobs that in practice were not performed as stand-alone jobs. Broadening the jobs had two important side effects: More training was required for employees to become proficient, and aptitude requirements for the new jobs increased. Both of these outcomes have important implications for HR systems because they place a premium on employee competence and ability.

Training Redesign

The technical training curriculum had to be revamped for several reasons. Training content has typically been built around specific and unique jobs. Because these jobs are all different due to the job redesign, training content had to change in response. There were also redundancies in the existing curriculum because different instructors prepared overlapping lessons. The new union agreement specifies that employees must pass training. Because some training materials had no terminal performance objectives (TPOs) and some were not pass-fail, more effort was required to make valid testing possible.

The training redesign has followed a modular philosophy similar to that of the FSR pilot discussed earlier. Almost every module is based on a task that each employee should be able to perform at the end of training. Training modules are targeted at lengths of two to four hours (though a few far exceed that), and a TPO generally specifies module content. Job knowledge tests are also an integral part of the new training modules, with test content tied directly to TPOs.

Two other aspects of the training redesign are critical here. First, instructional design adopted a "layers of necessity" instructional design model. This model is very pragmatic, recognizing that constraints like time, resources, budgets, instructor expertise, and preexisting training materials all bear on the level of detail and amount of training content that need to be developed. Second was the use of a rapid prototyping stage early in course development. This required each of the training design teams to produce a prototype module complete with TPO, training outline, and test items in about two weeks. All teams then viewed presentations of each others' products and jointly agreed upon one common design format.

Because training design is modular and modules are tied to tasks, it is easy to repackage training content as jobs evolve. If jobs change as a result of unbundling, for example, it will be simple to revise training to match. Another advantage of the modular design philosophy was that it made it possible to start the training redesign as soon as only a part of one of the new jobs was agreed upon, many months before completion of the job redesign process.

Applying the combination of modular training design, layers of necessity design philosophy, and use of rapid prototyping has paid off handsomely for SoCalGas. It is not uncommon for instructional design to consume 30 to 40 hours of staff time per hour of delivered training (American Society for Training & Development Benchmarking Standards). The average number of design hours per hour of delivered training for modules developed on this project is only about nine, a huge efficiency improvement. This achievement is even more impressive if one considers that over 400 training modules were developed and delivered in a nine-month period during 1996.

Testing

Testing development revolved around the major themes of training tests, selection tests, and automation of test scoring. After completion of the job redesign work, the company research staff analyzed the jobs using the PAQ. Jobs were then assigned to job families using the job slotting procedures, allowing the company to specify selection systems immediately. Selection tests covered cognitive aptitudes (reasoning, mathematics, mechanical aptitude, clerical aptitude, verbal skills) along with physical ability tests where needed. The research staff in coordination with training redesign completed the training tests. Most attention was focused at first on job knowledge tests. Hands-on (performance) tests and job knowledge tests used for bidders attempting promotion within progressions were under development in 1997 and later.

Before the reclassification project was undertaken, several selection systems had to be scored by hand, as did any tests used in training at that time. Much attention is now being focused on developing PC-based systems that allow scanning, scoring, and tracking of test data for applicants, bidders, and trainees. The same computer system will also generate feedback for test takers so they can focus their efforts on skills development.

Compensation

The compensation system has been dramatically altered to reinforce the job design philosophy. The number of pay grades dropped from 14 to eight, reinforcing the theme that both jobs and pay grades are now broader. The previous pay structure applied a series of eight step increases in each grade, which were tied only to the time a job was held rather than to job performance. In contrast, the new structure uses from two to four steps within a grade. Lump sums are awarded for significant increases in employee skill. These significant skill improvements are linked to passing required training and demonstration of proficiency on the job. The new structure allows either 24 or 36 months for movement to full proficiency (and full pay), depending on pay grade. Employees thus get the benefit of moving to full pay more quickly than under the old pay system, and the company gets the benefit of a more competent workforce. Because the new step and proficiency mechanism was designed to be cost neutral compared to the system it replaced, it results in a win-win situation for employees and the company.

Placement Process

The placement process for job bidders has also been drastically reworked. The union contract now requires selection tests for most jobs, ensuring better qualified candidates than under the old seniority-driven system. Bid priorities have been considerably reduced, from a high of over 40 to about five, which will allow more automation of bid processing. Employees can now bid for an unlimited number of jobs, but with the limitation that they can no longer refuse jobs they are offered.

Employees refusing a job for which they have bid now have all bids canceled, and they are prohibited from bidding again for one year.

These contractual changes in the bid process make it critical for employees to be sure they are truly interested in a job before they bid. The process also reinforces the need to upgrade one's skills and capabilities—a key element for the company's future success.

Skills Development Initiatives

The company has focused efforts on improving employees' basic skills with its Multimedia Learning Centers (MLCs) and on helping employees find jobs that fit them well through the Career Development Center. MLCs have dedicated PC workstations where employees can use software to help them evaluate their basic literacy skills and improve skills in reading, writing, and mathematics. MLCs also provide instruction on keyboarding skills and on PC software such as Windows, Word, and Excel. Future programs being planned for the MLCs include test-taking strategies and study guides for selection systems.

The Career Development Center is a new and evolving program that provides employees with opportunities to learn about their own interests and capabilities and about jobs both within and outside the company. Employees also get the chance to meet with a counselor to further explore jobs that meet their career goals. Future programs being planned for the Career Development Center will help employees even more in determining how well their skills, interests, and aptitudes match up with requirements of the newly redesigned jobs.

Consequences
Costs

The cost of developing and implementing the Reclassification Project was not recorded, other than the instructional design activities. As indicated earlier, the instructional design cost about nine hours of development for each hour of training produced, about 25 percent of a traditional design effort. The cost of planning the new jobs was reduced considerably by the cluster analysis and other analyses preceding the beginning of the project. The time required for training is by far the largest portion of the cost, but it is being spread out over more years than originally planned (about two). The benefit is that it is reducing the adverse impact on field performance by having too many employees in training and by trying to cope with a large proportion of inexperience in the workforce.

Results

Reclassification training had been in progress for six months as of early 1998. Union-management review teams approved the courses and tests with minor changes. Student performance in class has been largely satisfactory. The few failures were attributed to either inadequate preparation or poor literacy skills, not the training itself. At this point, the major hurdle is ensuring that every graduating student has an early opportunity to practice in the field what has been taught.

Evaluation Strategies

Evaluation has been limited to the training and so far has not encompassed the whole program. Evaluation is embedded in the training system. It includes new course tryouts using both reaction and test data (Kirkpatrick Levels 1 and 2). It is ongoing as the courses are repeated. Transfer data (Level 3) will be obtained later when proficiency evaluations are implemented, after the current phase of the program is complete.

Application of *The ASTD Models for Human Performance Improvement*

The foundations for this initiative took several years to develop, during which time SoCalGas underwent major shifts in management philosophy and business environment. What has been accomplished, however, maps well, post facto, on the ASTD model presented in *ASTD Models for Human Performance Improvement* (Rothwell, 1996). It has been a case of midlevel managers and their staffs drawing upon inferences from the business environment and moving ahead with pilot projects down a path dealing with some of the most tenacious underlying problems in the company.

In the following discussion, the steps of the ASTD model label each paragraph in which the corresponding activities undertaken at SoCalGas are described.

Performance Analysis

In the early 1990s, senior management became acutely aware that SoCalGas would face difficult times starting about 1994 if the company did not take immediate steps to change its cost structure and leverage its excellent relations with customers into a competitive force.

Consequently, the old, static management plan that emphasized having a smooth running system with captive customers was replaced by a more dynamic mission: putting customers first in a constantly changing, competitive environment. The business unit structure adopted in 1995 provided the new focus on customers and accountability for business results. Its objectives included substantially reducing costs and encouraging creativity to grow the business in a shrinking market. Because opportunities to provide additional company services were limited by regulation and many field employees were overly specialized, this shift in focus revealed major gaps: labor costs were not competitive with nonregulated businesses, excess workforce in some jobs could not perform work in high-volume jobs. One approach to closing this gap was to broaden the tasks technicians were qualified to perform, the approach discussed in detail in this chapter. The barriers to accomplishing this were formidable.

Cause Analysis

The incentive system for a traditional utility has its basis in the natural monopoly philosophy in which a state public utilities commission protects the company from competition while challenging its practices every few years to prove its rates are fair. Also, there is traditionally an implied job guarantee, which encourages people to make working at the utility a career, whether or not an individual is personally motivated to progress into more skilled work.

The union is well aware of a public utility's unique form of business. It has built up over the years certain expectations for its membership, encouraging overspecialization, protecting employees with light workloads, and downplaying the increasingly more technical nature of much of the work. The union's focus has been on processing grievances and leaving the concern for productivity to the company's management.

Training at SoCalGas developed in earlier times as people who performed the jobs taught them, and it has been updated by grafting in fixes. Looking at a traditional lesson plan today reveals little about what a student is supposed to be able to do at the end of training.

Finally, employees in technical jobs at SoCalGas have generally been well trained and highly experienced in their specialties. Evidence has been found, however, that there is less proficiency in basic skills (reading, writing, and mathematics) than had been presumed, and motivation to improve is often lacking.

Intervention

The starting point for the intervention was redesigning the field jobs, drawing upon findings from the cluster analysis of job data and knowledge of workloads and work distribution from managers of field operations. An important part of job redesign was compensation policy, which had to be structured to encourage participation and acquisition of new skills. Job design teams created job profiles from which training could be specified for both employees transitioning into the new positions and for promotion of employees into the new positions. The compensation system and proficiency evaluation system were designed to make sure the new workforce practiced what they had learned and to demonstrate they could handle more tasks. The union signed a letter of understanding to help seal the cultural change the company sought.

Implementation

Implementation of the reclassification training program was hampered by forces beyond the sphere in which human resources development personnel had influence. Three situations held the program back, slowing down the rate of training and eliminating some of the planned training. The situations were a delay in preparing field supervisors for changes resulting from the way the training would affect their work, a failure to take into account the loss of service if the training had adhered to the initial schedule, and extremely long delays by the union before it agreed to allow the training to proceed.

Change Management

There are several tools already in place to monitor change: the proficiency evaluations, actual workforce reduction (primarily through attrition), and evaluation of training. Customer satisfaction is also measured; however, in the first six months of implementation, it declined because of the first two problems.

Evaluation and Measurement

The success of a consultative approach to HR involvement in this project was most evident in the early stages: planning the job descriptions; developing the compensation, training, and proficiency subsystems; and setting up the computer-tracking system. Implementation, where HR could only advise and had little power to move the project forward, was less successful. Goals, priorities, and interests change over time, and apparently the two years spent on this project have taken their toll. The project continues but with lowered expectations and less long-term payoff. It has been successful, however, in bringing to life a new paradigm for HR at SoCalGas, in which a consultative approach can bring the wide range of skills together in a positive and creative way.

Conclusions, Learning, and Recommendations

SoCalGas has proposed, planned, and is implementing these broader nonmanagement jobs. Like the new HR systems, they are critical to the company's future. Although broader, more flexible jobs are an important element of this strategy, the new systems build upon and reinforce one another. The huge amount of progress made since the 1995 restructuring would not have been possible in the environment of even three years earlier. SoCalGas has made great strides in improving cooperation between departments and business units, in applying systems thinking, and in finding efficient and creative solutions to business problems. The company is also embarking on a new series of cooperative programs with its labor unions. The HR department has had a far greater impact in its new consultative role than in the administrative role that HR departments have traditionally played.

Questions for Discussion

1. Think of an industry with which you are familiar. What competitive advantage do organizations in that industry have and what social or environmental forces could erode the advantage?
2. What moves could human resources make to lessen the impact of those social or environmental forces on an organization's competitive advantage? (Use responses from question 1, if appropriate.)
3. This chapter distinguishes between the consultative and traditional administrative roles of human resources and advocates the consultative role. What are some attributes of that role? Discuss how they might strengthen the perception of human resources as a strategic resource?
4. Assume your human resources department wants to move to a consultative role as advocated in this chapter. What are some barriers within HR to making this change? What are some barriers within client and customer groups? What strategies can you employ to overcome these barriers?
5. On paper, conduct an informal needs assessment of human resources activities in an organization you are acquainted with, identifying gaps that impair productivity or generate avoidable costs. Identify possible solutions from this chapter, or other solutions that may occur to you, to reduce or eliminate those gaps.

6. At one time or another, the Southern California Gas Company has organized both central and decentralized human resources systems. What forces can enhance integration of the systems regardless of the degree of centralization and what forces can cause divisiveness and counterproductive behavior?

The Authors

Calvin Hoffman is employee development manager at the Southern California Gas Company. His staff is responsible for a wide range of human resources development activities including organizational and performance consulting, job analysis and job design, test development and validation, job evaluation, management training, instructional design, and PC skills training. He holds a B.S. degree in psychology from Kansas State University and M.A. and Ph.D. degrees in industrial/organizational psychology from the University of Nebraska. He is a member of the Personnel Testing Council of Southern California, the Society for Industrial and Organizational Psychology, and the American Society for Training & Development. He can be contacted at the following address: 8558 Lorain Road, San Gabriel, CA 91775.

John Stormes was introduced to instructional design in the mid-1960s, in the heyday of programmed instruction and wild prophecies about the power of multimedia. He wrote training materials and managed a variety of training development and behavioral science projects over the next 20 years, settling down finally in the training department of the Southern California Gas Company about 11 years ago. Here he has supervised the development of training video scripts and collateral material and has managed a number of sizable instructional design projects. He is currently instructional design supervisor and has recently been project manager of four instructional design teams redesigning all of the company's field training courses. He is a past president of the Los Angeles Chapter of the International Society of Performance Improvement. Stormes holds a B.S. degree in physics from San Diego State University and a B.A. degree (English) and an M.A. degree (cinema) from the University of Southern California.

References

Rothwell, W.J. (1996). *ASTD Models for Human Performance Improvement: Roles, Competencies, and Outputs.* Alexandria, VA: ASTD.

Solving Health-Care Performance Problems in a Turbulent Environment

General Hospital of Chicago

Joseph P. Yaney

This health-care service case involves interorganizational relationships, not traditional supervisor and employee situations. There are two sets of employees and two sets of organizational goals. Some goals are shared, but others are in conflict. This business case is about the nurses and laboratory staff who work with outside insurance adjusters on workers' compensation cases that can last a few days or a few years. For the hospital, such cases are extremely attractive and profitable. There is no collection problem because the insurance company is required to pay 100 percent of ordinary and reasonable fees. The insurance adjusters deal with many cases, just as the nurses deal with many patients. This creates a typical coordination problem to schedule visits, treatment sessions, and follow-up visits. The insurance adjusters have pressure to reduce costs, which may bring them in conflict with the hospital staff. Fortunately, there are accident cases with no conflicts because everyone agrees on what treatment is reasonable and ordinary.

Background

Urban health-care providers are facing many different problems. First, the public is losing patience with hospitals, physicians, and insurance companies. Health-care scandal after scandal is reported in the *Chicago Tribune* and other publications. Second, the environment is complex and unstable. Although it was once a calm environment in which different specialties were satisfied with their usual patient load, their compensation, and a more or less guaranteed future in-

This case was prepared to serve as a basis for discussion rather than to illustrate either effective or ineffective administrative and management practices. All names, dates, places, and organizations have been disguised at the request of the author or organization.

come, it has now changed to one of many adversaries. There are medical clinics saying that "so and so hospital staff" provided the wrong treatment, and more malpractice suits are being filed.

The environment is now unstable because physicians and other health-care providers are shopping around for the best deal. This act of disloyalty is now rampant in health care. Years ago the owners of the hospital might have had a standing committee on admitting privileges that the medical chief of staff chaired. Now the hospital president may be a certified public accountant and his or her chief lieutenant may be the vice president for marketing.

The insurance companies also operate in an unstable economic environment. Some executives of insurance companies were quoted in the *Wall Street Journal* as saying that they are paying out too many dollars in claims and that employees should return to work sooner. As the employee returns to work, this cancels the temporary total disability payments and may also slow down some physician bills.

This question of how much treatment is needed is a huge area of conflict. The hospital executives may argue that the patient needs more rehabilitation. The insurance adjusters are the boundary spanners for their companies. Although they may not be executives, the adjusters do interact with the employee's attorney, physician, case manager, and hospital accounting department. Without the insurance companies, the patients disappear.

Management and Employee Performance Issues

In this case at General Hospital of Chicago, the application of performance technology produced a better result than might otherwise have happened. Why? The executives and managers had started to isolate themselves into conference rooms debating whether there should be more pressure put on employees to work longer hours or whether more computer training would increase productivity. This is not unusual. Executives can be frustrated by economic and social problems and in a fit of poor judgment, they may just "do something." That something can be the wrong answer, which damages management decision making. Human performance technology offers a new set of ideas and action steps that shows respect for the executive's authority, but argues for patience and data gathering instead of confrontations.

Two Key Issues

The management issue is more complicated than the productivity issue. The first management issue hints that the way decisions are made may be suspect if subordinate managers are afraid to state their reservations about what the executives are proposing. The subordinates will be fearful of disagreeing with upper-level managers because they wonder whether they might suffer the results of executive disapproval, loss of status, or job loss.

The second issue can be seen in light of the human performance technology model. The productivity issue can be examined within a human performance technology framework. The human performance technology model and problem analysis is a much better solution than doing nothing and seeing the situation slip into a power fight between employees, supervisors, and executives. Most people do not want a power fight, but sadly there is evidence that some people do want a confrontation. The performance technology model seems acceptable to most executives and supervisors as a fair method to test alternatives before making a decision. That is, is there consistent evidence of some behavioral trouble, or is there perhaps mere grumbling?

This is a broadly stated question and one that needs some data collection and analysis before it can be answered. Stating the issue this way shows that the executives and supervisors are not acting hastily but are willing to invest some time and money in data collection. So there probably is a constant worry about being competitive, but no glaring problems. Past experience shows that reframing the issue around questionnaire information can avoid escalation of conflicts. If the questionnaires support some needed actions, then the changes can be made more calmly. If the questionnaires show employees understand and support management, then the executives can monitor the economic environment without having to do anything rash. The executives can feel relieved that when there is the usual grumbling, the employees understand that the outside environment of tough competition is the most important variable. The hypothesis at the hospital was that there might be room for productivity improvements, but it is not clear what can be done at this time.

How the Human Performance Technology Model Fits These Two Issues

The first issue involved preserving and enhancing the quality of management decision making. This is not the typical issue, but it is important nevertheless. Although the executives, management, and supervisors can use their formal authority to order changes, it makes more sense to ask employees to behave in a way most likely to succeed. Why? Service firms and health-care organizations have multiple tasks. Many people share the responsibility for patient care, so the problem analysis must ask if those individuals will voluntarily cooperate to deliver adequate nursing care.

The author's performance technology models ask about the job environment, the present level of behavior, cause-and-effect hypotheses, and how to gather new information, and then they require some intelligent speculation about whether the change effort will be worth all the time and money. In problem analysis, the environment includes the local history of who likes or hates which person, the quality of the equipment, the amount of working capital, and the competing departmental goals. The job environment is just plain unstable. What will the competing health-care providers do, for example? What will competing insurance companies do? The uncertain environment makes the employees, supervisors, and executives nervous. Studying the environment safeguards the parties from making incorrect assumptions, such as blaming individuals when the more likely explanation is that the whole market is declining. Blaming individuals is really asking for trouble. Instead, the consultant and the executives accept the reality of an unstable world. Today's answers might only be valid for six months, not forever. The parties need to monitor the environment to avoid being surprised by what is happening at the end of this six months. This viewpoint allows the supervisors and executives to hold a more balanced view that everyone faces work conflicts and that there is no employee conspiracy to cause trouble.

Section two of the performance technology model asks about what is happening today, what behaviors compared to what standards, and how much improvement is really possible. A higher standard has to make sense in terms of better medicine or being more competitive or some legitimate business reason. Health-care and insurance services are still vague. Just what is a higher standard of service? Some situations, such as accounting, might seem to be more straightforward. For instance, an analysis might show that employees have been making the same computing error because the employees did not understand how to operate the computer software. The answer, therefore, was to teach employees the software. That was a training example.

One of the lessons of this case is that there might be nontraining solutions that require the best thinking managers can bring to the table. There is a strong possibility that management might decide to leave things alone.

A Working Summary

The performance technology model embraces more ambiguity and more uncertainty than some training programs that had tighter scope and more easily measurable outcomes. Research consultants are not ashamed to say that they will gather more partial solutions, partial analyses, and tentative hypotheses before such complicated situations could be considered solved. The management decision issue is a sensitive political issue, not just a technical issue. The second issue of productivity sounds easier, but it is complex too because it includes individual employees, work groups, and group expectations. Good productivity studies always ask what is "fair" from the employees' viewpoint.

Problem Analysis and Data Gathering

The author's performance technology models start off using a broad-angle lens in viewing the potential problems. The consultant wants to examine the job environment, the present level of behavior, and the assumed cause-and-effect relationships. The first issue is about management's credibility and decision making. The consultant shares his thinking by talking to employees in small groups, drafting sample questions, and listening to the employees' stories about this job versus the competitor's way of doing things. These are all a part of touching and measuring how much or how little a problem might exist.

Problem analysis is similar to hypothesis testing—but the consultant will probably not use such specialized terminology with the clients. The first days are spent developing hunches and listening to employees. In performance technology, talking privately with employees and accumulating ideas are the first action steps. The organization will be changing because of the questions being asked. Expectations will be changing as employees watch what the executives are doing. The consultant knows that the local environment is not as positive as it was three years ago. Three years ago employers were willing to spend more money on health-care insurance and treatment. Private citizens were willing to pay the coinsurance dollars when choosing more and not less health care. The consultant knows that some hospitals are merging into provider chains and employees are losing their jobs.

The consultant is already thinking that maybe the parties should concentrate on low-cost steps.

Action Plans

One of the roles consultants play is to help the parties define what they see now and what might be changed. One tool that helps the parties is the employee-based questionnaire. The action plans typically stretch over a few months because of the need for supervisors and managers to approve the idea. Then the consultant designs, tests, and revises the questionnaire before distributing it. In this case, each employee in the health-care organization and in the insurance adjuster offices received a copy along with postage-paid envelopes for mailing the questions back to the consultant.

Working together with the liaison person and the employees, the consultant developed a questionnaire that tested specific ideas about how to improve performance (see an excerpt in figure 1). Through the results of a questionnaire, as well as through the dynamics created while designing, implementing, analyzing, summarizing, and disseminating the results, consultants can quietly advise the executives about what might be done or left alone.

Meeting with the Employees

The consultant in this case listened to the liaison nurse who was a boundary spanner between the hospital and the insurance companies. This liaison was quite helpful in understanding the areas of conflict within the insurance companies. The consultant understood that there was dissatisfaction over pay, hours, promotions, and required overtime work. The consultant wanted employees to feel comfortable expressing their views, but knew they had to be careful not to put themselves in risky situations at work by expressing unpopular views. The consultant and the liaison nurse looked for places to meet that were comfortable and confidential. Next, the parties helped the consultant create lists of ideas. For instance, were the employees interested in job sharing or job rotation? Were the supervisors interested in the same ideas? There was still the idea of having another computer workshop, so this item had to be in the questionnaire. The consultant was willing to listen to different viewpoints. Sometimes there were negative comments that told the consultant more about what had happened in the past. Management's credibility was explored in these questions:

You and Your Work Group
1 = strongly agree; 2 = agree; 3 = disagree; 4 = strongly disagree; 0 = DK, don't know
6. How much does your work group agree that top management makes the best marketing decisions when times are tough? *[1, 2, 3, 4, DK]*
7. How much does your work group agree that top management only cuts back when the economy is declining? *[1, 2, 3, 4, DK]*

Figure 1. Excerpt from an organizational research questionnaire.

Demographics

1. What is your gender? _____Female _____Male

2. What is your age? _____Years Old

3. What is your educational background? *(Check all that apply.)*
   - _____ High School Diploma
   - _____ Associate Degree
   - _____ Bachelor's Degree
   - _____ MBA
   - _____ Master's Degree (non MBA)
   - _____ Doctoral Degree

4. Marital status:
   - _____ married
   - _____ single with partner
   - _____ single (divorced)
   - _____ separated
   - _____ single (never married)
   - _____ single (widowed)

You and Your Work Group

(Please circle your response using the terms below.)

1 = Strongly Agree (SA)
2 = Agree (A)
3 = Disagree (D)
4 = Strongly Disagree (SD)
5 = Don't Know (DK)

Questions	SA 1	A 2	D 3	SD 4	DK
5. How much does your work group agree that top management makes the best marketing decisions when times are tough?	1	2	3	4	0
6. How much does your work group agree that top management only cuts back when the economy is declining?	1	2	3	4	0

continued on page 152

Figure 1. Excerpt from an organizational research questionnaire (continued).

Questions	SA 1	A 2	D 3	SD 4	DK
7. How much does your work group agree with top management's waiting a long time before rehiring personnel, as the organization's success is improving?	1	2	3	4	0
8. How much does your work group agree with the techniques and forecasts used by top management?	1	2	3	4	0

9. What obstacles will prevent you from receiving a pay increase or promotion? *(Please circle how much or how little each item prevented you.)*

1 = great deal	2 = much	3 = average	4 = not much	5 = very little

Questions	1	2	3	4	5
A little training	1	2	3	4	5
B people don't like you	1	2	3	4	5
C business declining	1	2	3	4	5
D too busy at home	1	2	3	4	5
E marital stress	1	2	3	4	5
F alcohol, drugs	1	2	3	4	5
G depression	1	2	3	4	5
H wrong education	1	2	3	4	5
I can't pay for more education	1	2	3	4	5
J few friends	1	2	3	4	5
K can't leave this town	1	2	3	4	5

10. Have you hit some troubled times? What type of support helped you gain a pay increase or a better job? *(Please circle how much or how little each item helped you.)*

1 = great deal	2 = much	3 = average	4 = not much	5 = very little

Questions	1	2	3	4	5
A time off to attend college	1	2	3	4	5

continued on page 153

Figure 1. Excerpt from an organizational research questionnaire (continued).

Questions		1	2	3	4	5
B	employer pays for computer courses	1	2	3	4	5
C	attending support group weekly	1	2	3	4	5
D	more religious time	1	2	3	4	5
E	trained counselor to help solve family conflicts	1	2	3	4	5
F	transfer to a new city	1	2	3	4	5
G	consultant improves your relationship with boss	1	2	3	4	5
H	outplacement helps you	1	2	3	4	5
I	lateral transfer to another job	1	2	3	4	5
J	job sharing	1	2	3	4	5
K	mentoring	1	2	3	4	5
L	better staff support	1	2	3	4	5
M	clearer work objectives	1	2	3	4	5
N	more accurate appraisals of your work	1	2	3	4	5
O	more creative assignments	1	2	3	4	5
P	more competent co-workers	1	2	3	4	5

11. If you would like to share a work story about yourself and your organization, please begin here:

Everyone liked the response options. If economic conditions were declining, both employees and supervisors were making the best of a difficult situation. Credibility was the key part of management issue number one. More ideas came across by asking if the employee conflicts could be negotiated or whether the situation was controlling. Are the employees stressed not only from work goals but also from not being able to give enough time to important relationships (family, children, marriage, and friends)? These competing goals were explored in the following question, which is excerpted.

What obstacles will prevent you from receiving a pay increase or promotion?
1 = great deal; 2 = much; 3 = average; 4 = not much; 5 = very little
A. little training? [1, 2, 3, 4, 5]
B. marital stress? [1, 2, 3, 4, 5]
C. alcohol, drugs? [1, 2, 3, 4, 5]
D. few friends? [1, 2, 3, 4, 5]

Discussions about competing goals are a time-honored part of problem analysis and problem solving. Poorly defined goals confuse the employees who want to coordinate their work.

The productivity issue (the second issue) consisted of three parts: how could management carefully allocate extra money to improve performance; what could the supervisors do to increase productivity; and what could increase employee motivation. The following questionnaire item reflects this focus on productivity:

Have you hit some troubled times? What type of support helped you gain a pay increase or a better job?
1 = great deal; 2 = much; 3 = average; 4 = not much; 5 = very little
A. time off to attend college
B. employer pays for computer course
C. consultant improves your relationship with your boss
D. better staff support

The next set of questionnaire items are about improving the working relationships between employees and supervisors.

What type of support helped you gain a pay increase or a better job?
[1, 2, 3, 4, 5]
A. clear objectives
B. creative work assignments
C. job sharing
D. lateral transfer

People spend a third of their lives at work. If they are fortunate, they earn enough to pay some bills and feel that they have helped other people. The consultant uses his hunches about what is happening in the work group. In this case, the consultant relied on the nurse liaison for feedback before typing the final draft of the report.

The third part of this productivity section is about the individual's self-perception. It is not an exact science, but an approximation of how employees see themselves. Some individuals see their strengths and weaknesses very clearly, whereas others are too frightened to see what is happening to them. Some issues are not one-shot ideas, but rather a pattern of behavior. One employee, the child of a bad marriage whom neither parent loves, for instance, may be worn down and unable to escape from his past that haunts and holds him back. Another employee, booming with self-esteem, decides that having an engineering degree is worth the time and sweat. That person may ask the employer to support his college education with tuition reimbursement and time off to attend class. The following question focused on this issue.

What type of support helped you gain a pay increase or a better job? [1, 2, 3, 4, 5]
A. attending a weekly alcohol or drug support group
B. a mentoring program
C. a weekly religious support group
D. a consultant to work with you and your supervisor to improve your relationship

Questionnaire Data

The employees gave their ages and educational background on page one of the questionnaire. The men had an average age of 38.6 years and the women about 42.6 years. About half of the people were married, and the other half were divorced or separated. All employees had additional education past high school and about half had a bachelor's degree.

Issue One: Management's Credibility

Management took heart that the employees believed that business conditions (more than management's poor judgment) restricted pay raises. This was rated a 2.8 on a five-point scale where 1.0 was the best score. The response was consistent with what the nursing liaison had said during the interviews. The employees were tired from working long hours. They did not have enough time for work and family, much less for taking college exams on the weekends.

Issue Two: More Training or Not?

The employees could give management feedback about what might be done with a few thousand dollars. The employees rejected computer training (it was a 4.3 score with 5.0 being a perfectly awful rating). Frustrated employees saw management's offer to give them more time for college courses as not very likely to help them get promoted (a 4.1 score on 5 scale with 5.0 being perfectly awful).

Issue Three: Relationship and Conflicts

Not everyone was happy with just completing the questionnaire. One middle-aged man wrote that he thought promotions came only from whom one knew and not from doing a good job. A laboratory specialist wrote that she felt abused when management forces her to work more overtime instead of hiring additional personnel. Her comment reflected the widespread feeling of not having enough time for family responsibilities.

The employees wanted clearer work objectives. The employees gave this questionnaire item a 2.9 rating with a 1.0 being in perfect agreement. The employees asked for more creative work. The creative work item received a 2.9 rating. Another item that mattered was having fair performance appraisals. The employees rated this a 2.7.

Issue Four: Some Alternatives for Management

The consultant had hoped that the employees would make suggestions that management could implement. They did in the next two items. First, the employees had a 3.1 rating for job sharing. This fit comfortably with the rest of the data that indicated that they felt a lack of time. Job sharing is spreading in all sectors, but especially in health care. Second, the employees asked for lateral transfers to a different job. This received a 2.8 rating with 1.0 being in perfect agreement.

Issue Five: Personal Motivation

The employees showed great courage in revealing personal problems. Psychological depression, alcohol, and drug abuse are tough issues. The females reported a 3.3 rating for feeling depressed with a 1.0 being in perfect agreement. The males reported a 4.0 rating for feeling depressed. Alcohol abuse was higher for the women at 3.4. The men showed a 3.8 rating.

If the employees could do self-analysis, the consultant wondered if a religious support group would be attractive. A specific item was added to the questionnaire. The response was a 4.3 with a 5.0 being in full disagreement with that idea.

Summary

The overall management goal was to protect the image of being fair and considerate leaders. This was part of their long-term strategy. The employees were understanding that outside economic pressures were real and not just being used as an excuse for not giving raises.

The questionnaire approach protected all the parties. Tough issues such as alcohol and drug abuse, being tired, and seeing few options all came out in the questionnaire. The employees understood that they had made mistakes in family responsibilities (divorces, separations).

The managers could put aside their half-hearted desire to conduct more computer-training classes because the employees did not want it. Second, these employees cannot leave their jobs whatever the disadvantages. They cannot leave family and just go to another city for a new job.

Questions for Discussion

1. Is this service organization similar to a factory? Can you build inventory for a rainy day?
2. What circumstances contribute to management's impatience and willingness to choose poor alternatives to seek productivity?
3. The executives chose to sit tight as a result of examining the questionnaire data. Does this mean that it was a waste of money to have hired the consultant?

The Author

Joseph P. Yaney is a consultant and professor working in the greater Chicago area. He has a doctorate in business administration from the University of Michigan. He also has a law degree and continues to do labor law consulting. His publications include a cost-of-training study published by ASTD. Yaney is a past national officer of the International Society for Performance and Instruction and is a frequent speaker at ASTD regional meetings. He can be contacted at the following address: The College of Business, Northern Illinois University, DeKalb, IL 60115.

References

Rothwell, W., and H. Kazanas. (1988). *Mastering the Instructional Design Process* (2d edition). San Francisco: Jossey-Bass.

Linking Performance Improvement to Cultural Change: One Organization's Story

AmeriGas Partners, LLP

Robert J. Rosania

This case illustrates one organization's successful attempt at improving the performance of its management team by redesigning key market-manager jobs to be more entrepreneurial; providing simulated real-world learning experiences to help instill newly defined performance expectations; and actively involving managers as participants in a large-scale effort to change the company culture.

Background

AmeriGas Partners, LLP, is the nation's largest retail propane marketer, serving more than 950,000 customers in 45 states. The company operates an extensive storage and distribution network using pipelines, barges, rail cars, and tanker trucks to transport propane to more than 600 local market distribution locations. To deliver propane locally to AmeriGas customers, the company uses over 2,000 bobtail trucks.

AmeriGas Propane, Inc., the general partner and operating company, is a wholly owned subsidiary of UGI Corporation, a 113-year-old supplier of natural gas and other energy services. With over 5,000 employees, AmeriGas serves residential, commercial, industrial, motor fuel, and agricultural customers, making up approximately 9 percent of the domestic retail market for propane.

In the spring of 1996, AmeriGas Propane enlisted the support of The Touchstone Partnership to help achieve its goal of improv-

This case was prepared to serve as a basis for discussion rather than to illustrate either effective or ineffective administrative and management practices.

ing the performance of its 120 market managers whose jobs had recently been redesigned to bring them closer to their customers. AmeriGas considered the achievement of this goal by the beginning of the next cold-weather season critical to the success of AmeriGas as it transformed itself from a highly centralized company to a more decentralized one.

With the restructuring of its business in the fall of 1995, AmeriGas's senior management created an organization where market managers, previously serving as single location managers, would be expected to act as general managers, responsible for four to seven districts. They also expected market managers to be more entrepreneurial and run their business as if it were their own. With the busy winter season fast approaching, however, little time was left to train these managers, who were in their positions just a few months, to perform their newly designed role. As a result, performance was not up to expectations, leaving all levels of management feeling frustrated, but determined to improve. Acting swiftly, this determination helped fuel the beginning of a dramatic organizational transformation.

Analysis

Recognizing the problem inherent in empowering employees without training them first, AmeriGas decided to develop a program to train all of these newly appointed managers in the basics of their job. The author, Robert "Bob" Rosania, a principal and senior consultant with The Touchstone Partnership, had been working with AmeriGas to develop a training strategy for the company. At the request of Diane Carter, AmeriGas's vice president of human resources, the consultants, Rosania and Skip Lange, led a process to design and develop this training with the goal of significantly improving market-manager performance.

To do this, the consultant, in the spring of 1996, began by first reviewing all of AmeriGas's previous attempts at assessing the performance needs of the market managers. Although somewhat helpful, the information proved to be incomplete because the position of market manager was so new. With a July deadline imposed by AmeriGas to begin the market manager training, the consultant knew that a formal and lengthy needs assessment was out of the question. Instead, he sought out the thoughts and opinions of those in the company most affected by the change. He began by interviewing senior executives, support staff, district managers, customer service representatives in the districts who were supervised by the market managers, and market managers, themselves. To gather data, the consultant asked a series of questions, including:

- Can you tell me about the organization from your perspective?
- What are your goals? How do they fit into AmeriGas's goals?
- What are some performance issues in the field as you see them? How can people's performance be improved in order to help meet AmeriGas's goals?
- What should market managers be doing to meet the organization's goals? What are they doing? What is preventing them from meeting the goals?

All the individuals interviewed were very candid in expressing their thoughts and concerns about the company and what was needed to enable it to grow. Interestingly, those in higher leadership positions seemed more apt to recognize the market manager as a key player in ensuring this growth. All seemed clear, however, that in a business where service is a key differentiator, those on the front line had to be fully trained to run their business as well as to understand and represent the company's values in meeting customer and organizational needs.

The needs assessment proved conclusively that in order for market managers to successfully perform their role in the organization and help achieve the company's strategic goals, they needed to be trained to perform in six areas directly related to the business. These areas of concentration were finance (later referred to as managing the business for profitability and growth), pricing strategies, customer focus, sales and marketing, people management, and safety. In addition, because AmeriGas aspired to function in a more team-based environment, together with the consultant it decided to add a team development component.

Once the consultant and AmeriGas identified these business-related areas, the consultant, with support from Diane Carter, who acted as program champion, convened an advisory council made up of AmeriGas executives, support staff, and market managers to verify the research and gain support, direction, and buy-in for what was to happen next. The advisory council, totaling 10 people, met for one day in late April. The challenge for what lay ahead quickly created an air of excitement that inspired even the most skeptical member of the group. After nearly a full day of discussion and give-and-take, the session concluded with the verification of the six areas of concentration as well as the formulation of a key objective: to develop a five-day learning experience that would create an environment where effective performance and enhanced business acumen would be in direct alignment with the achievement of companywide goals. Also on this day, the council gave the program its name, The Market Manager Forum.

Action

To accomplish this objective, Touchstone consultants began working with subject matter expert groups, led by champions, to develop training modules focused on five areas of concentration (the sixth, safety, would be under the leadership of an internal safety expert because the company was planning a major safety initiative in the near future). AmeriGas leadership chose training as the primary means for helping initiate the transformation of the company because most market managers were highly knowledgeable about the propane industry, but lacking in basic management skills. In an industry where traditionally most front-line managers came up through the ranks, it made sense to invest in in-house training for managers, rather than attempt to recruit them from other companies. In addition, AmeriGas viewed this as an excellent opportunity to deliver a consistent message regarding company expectations and goals to their entire management team in the span of just four months of training.

As the program development continued at a rapid pace, AmeriGas executives, excited about the opportunity to provide real business-related training for their market managers and, more important, begin the transformation of the company, raised an important question: "How can we be sure our managers will be able to transfer what they learned in the classroom back at their job?"

The consulting team had been thinking about this same question. Recognizing that what AmeriGas was about to embark on was less about training and more about a cultural change, the consulting team responded by incorporating a business simulation learning experience, specifically designed for AmeriGas, into the program. The advisory council quickly approved the idea and charged Skip Lange with the task of developing the simulation tool.

The consultant, now almost a member of the AmeriGas "family," with an office at corporate headquarters, knew the perfect person to work with Lange on developing the simulation. Bob Roseler, vice president and general manager for AmeriGas's western region, had spent some time with the consultant during a trip he had made earlier to Sacramento to learn more about the company. Roseler was an insightful and articulate person who seemed equally at ease teaching those around him as managing his region. The consultant knew he would be the ideal person to help provide the necessary context for the simulation. To provide assistance to Roseler and Lange, the advisory council asked Steve Sheffield, a market manager from New England, to be a part of the team to provide a real-world perspective to the simulation.

The consultant was now spending all of his time at AmeriGas helping plan the Market Manager Forum and how to get over 120 market managers through the program. Lange, meanwhile, was busy developing the training modules along with the simulation. As June quickly approached, arrangements were made to transport the market managers, some from as far as Alaska, to AmeriGas's headquarters in Valley Forge in groups of 24, over seven sessions (AmeriGas's leadership decided after the advisory council met that all region staff and some corporate staff would also attend, making the total number to be trained over 170 people). The company had already made arrangements at a local conference center to conduct the program and house the participants.

Under Lange's direction, the development of the modules would result in both participant and facilitator guides as well as visual aids containing program information. Because the advisory council had decided early on that AmeriGas senior managers would serve as the primary instructors for each module, the consultant designed and conducted a facilitator training program for the entire cadre of instructors the week prior to the first session. With the program materials developed and produced and all travel arrangements made, all that remained was to await the arrival of the first training group.

On Sunday, July 14, 1996, the first group of participants arrived at the conference center, anxiously awaiting the start of the first Market Manager Forum session the next day. To help welcome and assemble the group, a dinner and reception hosted by Gene Bissell, vice president of sales and operations, was held Sunday evening. Much of the talk at the reception centered on the fate of the people gathered in the room. Many wondered aloud whether they would be tested during the week to see who would get to stay and who would be asked to leave the company (this kind of talk seemed to subside in later sessions, as managers began to realize that the week in Valley Forge was for learning and not as a means for deciding who would be let go).

After an early morning breakfast at the conference center dining room, the first 24 participants filed into the training room, each wondering what the week would hold. Different color balloons were suspended from a chair placed at four different tables. These colors corresponded with color dots on each participant's name tag and represented four teams, made up of five to seven market managers and staff, who would go through the session together. At 8:00 a.m., Bob Rosania, serving as the resident coordinator and master of ceremonies, welcomed the group to the first Market Manager Forum.

At 8:10 a.m., the consultant introduced Lon Greenberg, chairman, president, and CEO of AmeriGas, to the group. Greenberg, who held the same titles at the parent company UGI, had just taken over the leadership of AmeriGas. He began by extending his greeting to the group and then quickly challenging them to use the coming week's experience as a means to help transform and reenergize the company. Greenberg's message was simple: "The company must change the way it conducted its business, and the people in the room were an integral part in making this happen." He then went a step further by explaining that through their efforts the market managers would, in effect, help establish the "new" AmeriGas.

Greenberg's message seemed to both inspire and intimidate some people in the room. As he left the floor, the purpose of the next five days began to crystallize in the minds of most who were seated in the audience. Although still somewhat unclear about how they were going to get there, most seemed to recognize the urgency of their leader's message that change was inevitable and, more important, that they were being asked to help lead the charge.

This approach of empowering managers to decide how to run their business was foreign to the "old" AmeriGas. After all, the company had traditionally been run with tight controls from Valley Forge. Now people would be given the responsibility for making decisions about how to run their market and, just as important, be held accountable for those decisions. This was all very new to those who were sitting in the room. Rather than spell out exactly how this change would be implemented, Greenberg was circumspect, implying that a formula for change would not be forthcoming in the session but that the necessary tools to help them perform and transform the company would be introduced as the next five days unfolded.

Lon Greenberg's message was reinforced by Paul Grady, vice president of sales and operations, who next addressed the group. Grady spelled out the company's new strategic goals and the purpose of the Market Manager Forum. He then presented "market manager critical success factors" and "key performance indicators," which would soon take effect, to help measure both company and market manager performance. Rather than issue them as an edict, Grady asked the group for feedback on whether the success factors and performance measures were appropriate given their new roles in the organization.

This provided the first real glimpse of the "new" AmeriGas—a senior official involving front-line managers in decisions that would have a direct impact on the company's future. In effect, Grady's invitation helped initiate the company's leadership and the participating managers in a process of dialogue that would extend for the rest of the week and would provide those in attendance with an insight into the new and emerging company culture.

After Grady's presentation came the training part of the program. It began with Dave Riggan, vice president of finance, leading the session called Managing the Business for Profitability and Growth. Riggan had a way of making a seemingly dry and intimidating subject, finance, come alive. His style of involving the audience helped create a learning environment where managers were free to participate and share "war stories" with one another.

As the class soon discovered, each subsequent facilitator, using his or her own unique style, worked hard at encouraging and supporting each manager to be an involved participant in the day's learning. The consultant had instructed the facilitators to follow the facilitator guide for their session, but were encouraged to add their own stories and examples to help make the instruction more meaningful and relevant for the participants. At the end of each day, the four teams received modules of the simulation to give them a chance to put into practice what they had learned.

The simulation was a "living case study" designed to mirror the real challenges market managers faced in the specific areas that the training covered. With each part of the simulation, teams had to make decisions about various issues. As the simulation ran its course, each team, operating at its own speed and level of cohesiveness, began to learn the importance of developing strategies and tactics to deal with the issues presented for the day. As the groups quickly discovered, working together as a team proved to be easier said than done.

Once the simulation began, the consultant told each team that its goal for the session was to solve the "problem" in the simulation and be prepared to present the "solution" to a panel of senior executives on the last day of the session. Because there was no one best solution, each team would have to rely on its own ingenuity to draw upon each member's expertise and experience as well as the members' ability to work as a team, incorporating what they learned in the classroom to arrive at their solution to the problem. To help create even more interest, prizes would be awarded for the best "solution" to the simulation. Because the teams were made up of individuals who had never worked together, much less knew each other, mini-instruction sessions on working effectively as a team and making a presentation, led by Bob Rosania and Penny Zimmerman, manager of employee and organization development and AmeriGas's on-site coordinator, were offered throughout the week.

As the groups began to coalesce (some better than others), a competitive spirit began to develop between them. Some of the more inventive teams figured out ways to locate laptop computers to aid in solving the simulation (after session 1, each group received laptops). By midweek, some team members were talking about how they were working well into the night on the simulation. This talk served to ratchet up each team's desire to solve the simulation and make the best presentation. When groups got bogged down, they were encouraged to seek out help from Bob Rosania and Penny Zimmerman, who served as on-site "coaches."

As the groups continued to work, many late into the night, some elements of the new AmeriGas began to emerge. Managers began to view "Valley Forge corporate types" in a somewhat different light. These were not people intent on making life miserable for employees in the field. Rather these were colleagues, acknowledging the need for change in running the business, as well as teachers unafraid to admit that they did not have all the answers. These were people, who, like them, were struggling with issues around securing AmeriGas's future. Only now they were offering the market managers a real stake in ensuring AmeriGas's standing as "America's Propane Company."

On the final day of the session, each team gave its presentation to a panel of three or four senior executives. The teams had been told previously that they would be allowed no more than 20 minutes to present and that they could be as creative and inventive in developing and delivering their presentation as they wanted. The winner of the simulation competition would be the team that presented the best solution to the simulation as judged by the panel. Because no right solution actually existed, the criteria used to judge the teams included teamwork, innovation, presentation skills, and, most important, the appropriate use of the tools, concepts, and skills presented during the five days of the program.

As the four teams filed into the room, what had begun three months earlier as an idea for a management training program for 120 market managers had clearly taken on new meaning. Despite the fact that there was much more left to do, this was indeed the beginning of the new AmeriGas culture; one where Valley Forge executives would share the spotlight and work hand-in-hand with managers in the field.

As expected, the quality of presentations and solutions ran the full spectrum from somewhat off target to illuminating and worthy of further consideration outside the program. The caliber of solutions improved and presentations seemed more polished as the series of seven sessions continued throughout the summer. Some managers in later sessions acknowledged having been warned that their stay would be "no party" and that only through hard work and "out-of-the-box thinking" could they expect to impress the panel. Stories began to circulate about all-night work sessions getting prepared for the Friday presentation. These stories and the demanding schedule of the program are still referred to today and now serve as part of the company lore. Another interesting phenomenon revolves around the executive panel. Despite extremely busy schedules, as word of the Market Manager Forum spread, more and more senior managers asked to participate on the panel. Amazingly, Dave Riggan, the vice president of finance and forum instructor who is known throughout Ameri-Gas for putting in long hours, insisted on serving on the panel for all seven sessions.

In every session, the executive panel provided each team with constructive feedback about its solution and the reasoning behind their decisions. Consultants also encouraged panel members to question the groups regarding the "whats," "whys," and "hows" of their solution as well as how effectively they felt the week's session had prepared them to work through the simulation. The time spent giving and receiving feedback was valuable because all four teams were in the room during the presentations and feedback sessions and were able to learn from one another.

For each session, each member of the team that had been judged as having the best solution received a certificate and limited edition marble "bobtail" truck as its prize. When earned, certificates were also awarded for runner-up and most creative solutions. More important than any prize awarded during any of the seven sessions, however, was the effect working together toward a common goal had on the participants. In a company whose growth has been primarily through acquisition, company values rarely supported cooperation with someone who might have been your competitor the day before. In this experience, though, these barriers began to crumble as each manager began to realize that his or her success would be ensured only if the group was successful. As the new AmeriGas continues to emerge, this lesson can be seen played out in markets in small towns throughout the country.

Evaluation

In all, over 170 managers and staff participated in the inaugural Market Manager Forum, during seven sessions from July through October 1996. The results of the Market Manager Forum are best measured by evaluating the following hard and soft anecdotal data.

One way is by measuring perceptions of participants in the program. Through formal evaluations for each module and the program in its entirety, participants gave an overall rating of 4.27 for all seven programs, with one being the lowest and five being the highest. Many participants commented in their evaluation of the program that their experience with the simulation helped challenge old ways of thinking about their role as a manager. As one manager put it, "It stretched my capabilities...got me to think and use skills that I might not otherwise have used—it was a great learning experience."

A second, more important way to evaluate the effectiveness of this experience is by looking at improved performance as reflected in people's ability to do their job and meet company goals for profitability and growth. Although difficult to measure, there is some strong evidence indicating improved performance among the market managers who participated in the program. In the year following the first Market Manager Forum, the turnover rate for market managers was fairly high. Because most had never managed more than one location before, many struggled with the complexities of being a multi-location general manager despite their intense training. As a result of this turnover, and with continuing emphasis on coaching and training, those who are currently in the market manager position are exhibiting greatly improved levels of performance.

Evidence of that is that AmeriGas's financial performance improved considerably in the fiscal year following the training. Despite weather that was 7 percent warmer than in 1996, earnings before interest, taxes, depreciation, and amortization increased 28 percent; net income increased 330 percent; and distributable cash flow increased 52 percent. In the company's annual report for 1997, Lon Greenberg, AmeriGas president and CEO, states:

> We have dedicated this year's annual report to our employees. We have done so to recognize their outstanding contributions in helping us achieve improved performance in fiscal 1997 and their firm resolve to assist us in achieving our potential in the future.... I see an inseparable link between financial success and the way an or-

ganization views its people. As I travel to our field locations, I am continually impressed with the commitment of our employees. Their efforts to satisfy our customers and their patience as we navigate the changes necessary to make our business more competitive are commendable. We are committed to doing more for our entire employee team. Each dollar we invest—in their training, in safety equipment, in performance incentives—is a dollar invested in the growing success of our firm.

Although the improved financial performance and employee efforts to support change cannot be linked directly to participation in the Market Manager Forum, to suggest that their was no relationship would be equally far-fetched. One way of measuring the success of any cultural change effort is through the observations of those experiencing it. Perhaps this is best illustrated by AmeriGas's vice president of human resources, Diane Carter, who stated: "By focusing the AmeriGas simulation around real issues facing the company at that time, the participants were able to develop solutions that they could take back to their own areas of responsibility. Giving the managers the chance to work with colleagues from different parts of the country, as well as functional managers from headquarters, stimulated fresh 'out of the box' ideas for individuals who may have done their jobs the same way for years."

As a postscript, since the completion of the Market Manager Forum in October 1996, market manager Randy Hannigan has been promoted to vice president and general manager. Hannigan had proved himself in many ways in the past, but the training program had given him more visibility at headquarters. He was selected from among several market managers, all of whom the leadership at AmeriGas had come to know at the training.

Since the completion of the Market Manager Forum, AmeriGas has conducted an equally successful Market Manager Forum II, focusing primarily on the issues of safety and people management. The company has also extended training to supervisors in the corporate functions and has implemented a succession planning process, using a multirater 360 feedback tool. Although AmeriGas continues to measure and reward market managers on the financial performance of their market and growth in the business through increased volume and customer growth, it is now also measuring them on performance against the key performance indicators that they helped develop in the program.

Questions for Discussion

1. Given the context that AmeriGas is changing its culture, what are the pros and cons of awarding prizes for the best "solutions" to the simulation during the Market Manager Forum?
2. How could the lessons about "teamwork" be reinforced during the Market Manager Forum? After the Market Manager Forum?
3. What strategies would you implement to determine the business impact of the Market Manager Forum?
4. In addition to the Market Manager Forum, what are the other factors that may have influenced the improvements in the financial performance of AmeriGas? Would these other factors tend to have a greater influence than the forum? How would you know?
5. How would you relate the efforts of the forum to determine its business impact and the impact of the other factors?
6. What issues will AmeriGas management need to continue to address in order to influence a successful change effort? What should be management's role in continuing to address these change issues? When (time frame) can they expect the change effort to be completely successful?

The Author

Robert J. Rosania, a principal with The Touchstone Partnership, Ltd., is a successful human resources development professional with over 18 years of experience working with organizations to improve manager, leader, and employee performance. He has provided support for clients in the financial services, energy, and service management industries as well as in government. Rosania has extensive experience in the areas of program design, development, and presentation, emphasizing behavior change and performance improvement. He has served as an adjunct instructor in psychology at Mercer County (New Jersey) Community College and in Leadership and Motivation at The Pennsylvania State University. His special interest and expertise in the subject of work/life balance has led to frequent appearances on local radio shows in Philadelphia. Rosania has an M.A. degree from Seton Hall University and a B.A. degree from the University of Dayton. He has studied family therapy at The Trinity Counseling Center in Princeton and completed coursework at The Institute for Human Relations Training in New York. He can be contacted at the following address: The Touchstone Partnership, Ltd., 997 Old Eagle School Road, Suite 201, Wayne, PA 19087. He can be reached at e-mail: brosania@aol.com; phone 610.687.2525; or fax: 610.687.2756.

Human Performance in Action: The NASD'S CORNERSTONE

National Association of Securities Dealers

Andrea K. Moore and Deborah L. Stone

The following case study describes the CORNERSTONE™ project, which the National Association of Securities Dealers (NASD) and DLS Group, Inc., (DLS) designed, developed, and implemented. In the beginning of the project, the client focused on a specific media type, rather than the performance problems of the target population. However, after extensive collaboration, including discussions on the performance support chain, the NASD realized that a flashy, state-of-the-art multimedia training program would not provide it with the financial returns and improved performance it desired. In the end, CORNERSTONE realized those goals through reduced time to master the job, reduction in rework, improved employee satisfaction, and improved customer satisfaction, among other ways.

Background

In 1992, the National Association of Securities Dealers found itself in an enviable position. Its exponential growth rate over the past two decades made it the world's leading self-regulatory organization (SRO) in the securities industry, with oversight responsibilities for more than 5,000 member firms and 500,000 securities professionals (Villachica & Stone, 1998).

Growth generally leads to increased training needs, however, and this case was no exception. Although its examiner training program was generally considered one of the best in the industry, novice examiners needed approximately two years to become proficient at their

This case was prepared to serve as a basis for discussion rather than to illustrate either effective or ineffective administrative and management practices.

jobs. The ever-changing nature of the industry itself was partially to blame for the time needed to achieve job mastery. "Our industry is governed by volumes of complex standards, rules, and regulations that are updated and amended constantly as new products, trends, and practices emerge," said John Pinto, executive vice president of NASD Regulation, the enforcement arm of the NASD (Villachica, 1996).

When the NASD first contacted DLS, a performance enhancement consultant in Denver, Colorado, it had one overriding objective—train a large number of new examiners in a reduced amount of time. The NASD also had a vision of how to do so. It was particularly interested in using computer-based training (CBT) and multimedia to reduce the training time necessary to acquire examiner mastery (Kulik, Kulik, & Shwalb, 1986).

Initial discussions with DLS identified a number of performance problems that could not be solved by increased multimedia training, however (Villachica & Stone, 1998). Using the human performance technology (HPT) principle of a performance support chain, DLS determined that the NASD had a number of potentially broken links that contributed to the skill and knowledge deficiencies. Accepting DLS's advice that training alone might not solve its business problems, the NASD requested a needs assessment prior to making a final decision regarding the type of training it would enlist. The primary purpose of the needs assessment would be to identify significant gaps in performance, specify their sources, and formulate preliminary interventions to close the gaps.

The results of the needs assessment confirmed the preliminary diagnosis—a systematic solution was the best way to improve organizational and individual performance and repair the performance support chain. Over the next three years, the NASD and DLS would create CORNERSTONE, one of the largest performance support systems of its kind, consisting of 21 components and 10 types.

Organizational Profile

One of the primary responsibilities of the NASD's approximately 550 examiners is to conduct annual and special audits of securities firms throughout the United States to ensure that they are complying with financial and sales practice regulations. NASD examiners are located in 11 district offices throughout the continental United States, with an average of 50 employees per district. Although many firms are located in the cities in which the 11 district offices reside, examiners must travel to other member firms to conduct their exams. Depending on the type of exam they were conducting, examiners were required to bring suitcases full of background information and support documentation—a cumbersome process that is prone to errors and inconsistency.

One reason so much documentation was necessary was the scope of the NASD's jurisdiction. The NASD's purview extends to every activity and product with which an NASD firm is involved, including stocks, bonds, municipal funds, and derivatives, among others. The condition of the stock market also has a significant effect on the NASD and the exams it conducts. Typically, when the market is strong, more products are introduced and, in turn, more exams needed. Initiatives such as SEC mandates and organizational restructuring also influence the number of exams. In other words, as the market grew, the need for exams became greater and more complicated.

At the time of this effort, the NASD was not constrained by the number of examiners it could employ. It was limited, however, by a learning curve of two and one-half years for new examiners to reach mastery. The NASD realized that by reducing the amount of time for a new employee to learn the job, productivity would increase. Moreover, many opportunities existed to improve the productivity and performance of the existing staff. Across the organization, the NASD was interested in improving performance for both its new and existing examiners.

Target Population

During the needs assessment, DLS investigated three levels of performers:

- *Novice examiners,* which consisted of examiner trainees and associate examiners who had been on the job less than 18 months. Most novice examiner backgrounds were in the securities, banking, or accounting arenas.
- *Competent examiners,* which consisted of compliance examiners and senior compliance examiners who had been on the job more than 24 months.
- *Subject matter experts,* which were examiners recognized for excellence. They had conducted or participated in a number of complex examinations with superior results.

All NASD examiners can be categorized as knowledge workers. In general, knowledge workers are people who perform jobs that regularly require them to solve problems. To this end, they possess complex, domain-specific knowledge and skills, which do not readily transfer to other unrelated jobs or tasks. Knowledge workers use continuously changing information. Although these individuals have internalized large amounts of information, they also regularly access external information as they need it. In short, knowledge workers possess and use vast amounts of information to conduct complex reasoning activities such as collecting data, weighing evidence, drawing conclusions, making deductions, and articulating rationales (Stone & Villachica, 1997).

For NASD examiners, this type of problem solving is not an occasional necessity, it is an integral aspect of a routine day's work. Problems arise when examiners have goals they do not know how to achieve. Some of these problems are well structured. Experienced examiners identify the problems, develop straightforward processes for solving them, and know what the solved problems will look like. Other problems are ill structured. Even the most experienced examiners cannot necessarily identify the problem at the start, they don't know exactly how to solve it, and they don't know what it will look like when they are done (Stone & Villachica, 1997). But what makes experienced examiners experts is their ability to transfer the knowledge they have solving the well-structured problem and apply it to solving the ill-structured problem.

Key Players

The creation of CORNERSTONE, was a collaborative effort of the NASD and DLS. To this end, NASD personnel filled the following roles during the needs assessment and development phases of this project:

- *Stakeholders:* executive vice president of the NASD's regulatory wing (key stakeholder and process owner), as well as vice presidents and directors of other NASD organizational groups.
- *Examiner training steering committee (SC):* directors and training directors, counsel, associate district directors, and the NASD CORNERSTONE, project manager. This group was responsible for establishing the overall direction of CORNERSTONE, resolving open issues, and specifying the best practices CORNERSTONE would address.
- *Technical review teams (TRTs):* novice and expert examiners, supervisors, liaisons to the NASD's corporate training group and steering committee, and the NASD CORNERSTONE project manager. These groups were responsible for working with DLS to specify technical requirements, formulate design approaches for meeting those requirements, and review all draft materials for technical accuracy, relevance, and appropriateness for the examiner population.

- *Subject matter experts (SMEs):* selected on the basis of being a technical expert as well as an opinion leader in the examiner community. To accommodate a variety of technical perspectives, provide a venue for resolving potential SME disputes, and specify initial best practices, two or three SMEs supported each component.
- *Examiners:* appropriate mixes of novice, experienced, and expert examiners participated in usability and pilot tests, and as subjects during the needs assessment.

Because of the breadth of the performance support system, DLS employed human performance technologists, instructional designers, systems analysts, human factors engineers, graphic designers, programmers, documentation specialists, and authoring specialists as well as DLS's own internal securities subject matter experts. Recognizing that the project's size warranted a full-time project manager, DLS assigned an experienced project director as the leader and key project member for this effort.

The CORNERSTONE Initiative: Chronology, Issues, and Events

The CORNERSTONE effort consisted of two phases: a needs assessment and a development phase. Although not initially planned as a phased project, the project moved in that direction at DLS's recommendation and the NASD's realization that an online multimedia training program could not fix all of its examiners' performance problems.

The Needs Assessment

DLS's first strategy for providing performance support for examiner knowledge workers was to identify and resolve systemic gaps in performance. All too often, organizations employ subsystem solutions to address systemic problems, with little or no results (Stone & Villachica, 1997). This was, in fact, the solution the NASD first proposed with its multimedia CBT solution. As previously discussed, individuals unfamiliar with systematic human performance technology solutions might attribute the NASD's performance gaps solely to a skill and knowledge deficit, which a technology-based, self-paced training course could solve. The inherent problem with this solution is that performance gaps often result from multiple, interacting sources. These interacting sources can be categorized by different links in the performance support chain, as figure 1 shows. In this chain, fixing one link does not necessarily repair other broken links.

During the needs assessment, DLS personnel spoke with NASD managers and project stakeholders to specify critical success factors,

Figure 1. The performance support chain.

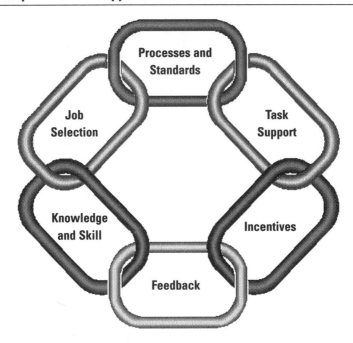

interviewed 20 SMEs to begin specifying the mental model they used to conduct examinations, and conducted focus groups with less-experienced examiners to identify gaps in their knowledge and skills. In all, DLS contacted 103 examiners, comprising approximately one-third of the total population. Table 1 summarizes the performance gaps and sources that DLS identified during the needs assessment (adapted from Villachica & Stone, 1998).

The needs assessment uncovered the following five significant business problems:

- Novice examiners needed to master their jobs in 50 percent less time. Before CORNERSTONE, novice examiners required over two years to master their jobs, primarily because of the complexity of the required skills and knowledge, along with the relative invisibility of the cognitive processes involved. With an examiner's average job tenure being approximately five years, up to half of an examiner's time at the NASD could be spent coming up to speed.
- Examiners needed to keep better pace with changes in securities products and regulations. Prior to CORNERSTONE, examiners had to create and maintain their own libraries to keep pace with changes

Table 1. NASD performance gaps and sources.

Performance Gaps	Sources
Novice examiners needed to master their jobs in 1.5 years, not 2.5.	• Novices lacked the skill and knowledge necessary to perform their jobs. • Novices lacked access to just-in-time, on-demand training, information, and advice that would enable them to master their jobs in the shortest possible time period.
Experienced examiners should remain in their jobs with the NASD for more than 2.5 years.	• Experienced and expert examiners lacked adequate opportunities for further advancement within the organization.
Examiners should keep pace with rapid changes in securities products and regulations.	• Examiners lacked just-in-time, on-demand access to timely, well-organized, standard information about securities products and regulations.
Examiner training should adequately prepare novice examiners to perform their jobs.	• Examiners who completed training lacked procedural skills and knowledge they could transfer to the job. • Mentors lacked organizational support to perform their jobs. • Mentors lacked the skills and knowledge to perform their jobs. • Mentors lacked the materials to perform their jobs.
The modules (form-based job aids) that examiners complete when they conduct exams should be current and easy to use.	• Examiners lacked appropriate just-in-time, on-demand tools for completing the exam modules and writing their reports. • Examiners lacked the most recent modules they needed to conduct exams because a systematic method for updating modules did not exist.

Source: Villachica, S.W., and D.L. Stone. (1998). "CORNERSTONE: A Case Study of a Large-Scale Performance Support System." In *Performance Improvement Interventions: Methods for Organizational Learning*, volume 3, Peter J. Dean and David E. Ripley, editors. Washington, DC: International Society for Performance Improvement. Reprinted with permission of the International Society for Performance Improvement.

in securities products and regulations. In addition to taking time from other job tasks, these personal libraries varied widely in quality and often led to uneven job performance. Moreover, the questions experienced examiners commonly ask to identify the critical features of securities products had not been captured. As a result, examiners typically suffered from "information bulimia," a state where they alternately had too much or too little information (Rossett & Gautier-Downes, 1991), and the information itself was often difficult to access.

- NASD has not captured or disseminated the cognitive decision processes or mental models that expert examiners used to conduct examinations. The decision processes that expert examiners use to conduct examinations had never been documented. There were no written standards for conducting exams, nor was the NASD capturing its best practices and leveraging them across the entire organization.

- Examiner training did not adequately prepare examiners to perform all aspects of their jobs. Although the NASD's training was generally recognized as the best in the industry, examiners reported that their instructor-led courses did not sufficiently prepare them for the job. Examiners who had completed the existing training still lacked the skills and knowledge they needed to perform their jobs.

- The paper-based forms (examination modules) that examiners used to conduct exams were often out of date, cumbersome, and time-consuming to use. The ever-increasing size and complexity of the exam forms made them difficult for novice examiners to complete and cumbersome for all examiners to use. Stacked on top of each other, a complete set of forms reached three feet in height. Using these forms, novice examiners tended to overanalyze unimportant (but obvious) problems and underanalyze important (but subtle) ones. The reports examiners wrote on basis of the completed forms also varied widely in format and quality.

In summary, the needs assessment identified a number of complex and interrelated performance gaps including environmental, motivational, feedback, performance standards, and skill and knowledge gaps. Clearly, these performance gaps were systemic in nature and could not be solved with isolated interventions. NASD did not need to solve isolated gaps in performance; rather, it needed a large-scale, integrated performance support system (Villachica & Stone, 1998).

The Development Phase

Once DLS completed the needs assessment, and the NASD accepted the performance support system (PSS) recommendation, the

NASD prioritized the potential solution recommendations documented in the needs assessment report. The CORNERSTONE solutions as they relate to the detected performance gaps are documented in table 2.

The first step in the development phase was determining the mediums that would best close the specified performance gaps. Because the problems facing examiners were diverse, their solutions would require varying levels of feedback, extrinsic motivation, and simulation. In an extensive collaborative effort (as described in the Models and Techniques section), the NASD and DLS analyzed the high-level issues relating to the training and information requirements, and how these requirements would affect the examiner population. The output of these analysis sessions was a preliminary curriculum map, as depicted in figure 2 (adapted from Villachica & Stone, 1998).

Following selection of the medium, the NASD and DLS were ready to begin the analysis and design of the various components. Although countless decisions affected CORNERSTONE, four primary events shaped its final design and eventual implementation:

- *Using cognitive apprenticeship techniques within the online types of medium.* In the training field, specifically in instructor-led training, cognitive apprenticeship is not a new methodology. It is new, however, when teaching or presenting information in an electronic capacity. On the basis of conversations about methods that were successful for novice examiners in their current training, the NASD and DLS determined early in the design process that cognitive apprenticeship approaches would be appropriate for the examiners. One aspect that novice examiners liked about their existing instructor-led training was the "war stories" from the instructors. Novice examiners believed that this instructional method, more than any other classroom experience, accurately depicted their roles and responsibilities. New examiners also liked having access to their instructor "mentor" to ask questions and receive advice.

The specific challenge created by the decision to use cognitive apprenticeship teaching methods—specifically modeling, coaching, scaffolding, articulation, and reflection—was how to incorporate it within the CBT. The implementation of the design proved to be no easy task. Because models or examples did not exist, the NASD and DLS were pioneering the design for online cognitive apprenticeship. The methodology chosen, and the one that ultimately made this experimental effort successful, was prototyping. Prototyping, a collaborative analysis and design technique, enabled DLS to create successive approximations of the final design. These iterations, which increased in scope and complexity, allowed the NASD to see

Table 2. NASD performance gaps, potential interventions, and CORNERSTONE solutions.

Performance Gaps	Potential Interventions	CORNERSTONE Solutions
Novice examiners needed to master their jobs in 1.5 years, not 2.5.	• Reduce time to job mastery by creating a training path that would provide novice examiners on-demand, just-in-time access to the skill and knowledge required to perform the job.	• Self-paced foundations training • Electronic performance support system (EPSS) • CBT • On-the-job training
Experienced examiners should remain in their jobs with the NASD for more than 2.5 years.	• Close motivational gaps for experienced examiners by creating a formal, career-advancing responsibility as mentor. • Provide the training, resources, and release time mentors need to meet this responsibility.	• Mentoring and on-the-job training • Instructor-led mentor training
Examiners should keep pace with rapid changes in securities products and regulations.	• Allow examiners to access the volatile information they need online. • Provide a single, timely source of information that describes securities products and regulation.	• Hypertext product information • Automated examination modules (AEM)
Examiner training should adequately prepare them to perform their jobs.	• Foster transfer to the job by creating a training path for novice examiners that employs performance-based training, simulations, scaffolding, timely hints from mentors, cognitive apprenticeships, and situated cognition. • Specify a mentor selection program, and provide mentors with release time to work with their protégés. • Provide training so mentors possess the skills, knowledge, and materials to perform their jobs.	• Self-paced foundations training • EPSS • CBT • Mentoring and on-the-job training • Instructor-led mentor training

The modules (form-based job aids) that examiners complete when they conduct exams should be current and easy to use.

- Create a custom software tool examiners could use to complete the exam modules and write the first draft of their final exam reports.
- Provide module forms online so that all examiners always have the most recent information.

- Automated examination modules

Figure 2. Preliminary curriculum map.

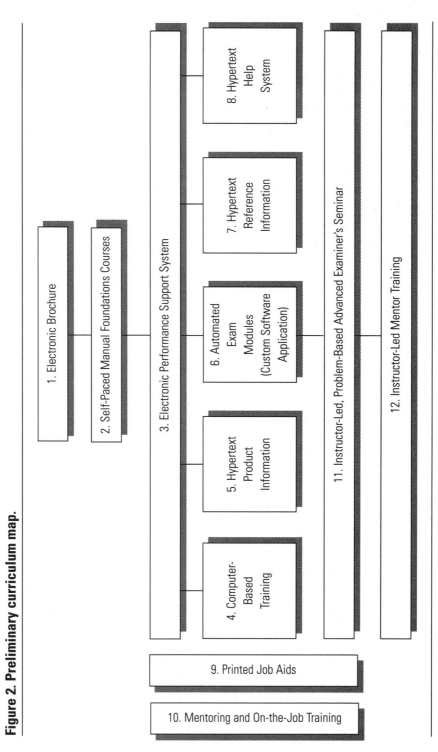

1. Electronic Brochure

2. Self-Paced Manual Foundations Courses

3. Electronic Performance Support System

4. Computer-Based Training

5. Hypertext Product Information

6. Automated Exam Modules (Custom Software Application)

7. Hypertext Reference Information

8. Hypertext Help System

9. Printed Job Aids

10. Mentoring and On-the-Job Training

11. Instructor-Led, Problem-Based Advanced Examiner's Seminar

12. Instructor-Led Mentor Training

Source: Villachica, S.W., and D.L. Stone. (1998). "CORNERSTONE: A Case Study of a Large-Scale Performance Support System." In *Performance Improvement Interventions: Methods for Organizational Learning*, volume 3, Peter J. Dean and David E. Ripley, editors. Washington, DC: International Society for Performance Improvement. Reprinted with permission of the International Society for Performance Improvement.

a representation of the cognitive apprenticeship methods and provided it with a context from which to formulate comments and suggestions. Without prototyping, designs would not have been as complete, nor would they have been as timely.

- *Capturing organizational knowledge.* Prior to CORNERSTONE, the NASD had never attempted to capture its organizational expertise. Acquiring and codifying this expertise from over 100 experienced examiners proved to be a challenge. The experts were both skeptical about the value of collecting the organization's best practices, and they had many different ideas about what those best practices were. To overcome these obstacles, the design team recommended that the project stakeholder, the executive vice president of regulation, take the prototypes out in the field to demonstrate a preliminary design. This step provided examiners not only with a visual representation of an expert's best practice but also with a look at the top executive in the department's commitment and dedication to the project. By demonstrating that the organization was serious about embracing change, the examiners were informed that their support was expected and required.

  Capturing organizational knowledge proved easier than initially anticipated. Although many of the experts believed their methods were unique, the design team discovered most of them followed the same basic model. The differences typically involved the way in which the experts articulated the model, rather than the model itself. Expert examiners demonstrated textbook expert behavior: much of the knowledge that makes up expert performance is invisible (Villachica & Stone, 1998). To make it visible, the NASD and DLS used the collaborative analysis and design techniques of joint requirements planning (JRP) meetings and joint application design (JAD) meetings. JRPs and JADs bring the design team and the SMEs together to discuss requirements and design issues. The design team's goal was to include SMEs with varying opinions about the work processes. The team understood that for every expert, there is an equal and opposite expert. Although in most instances, the experts discovered that semantics proved to be the primary disagreement, other true disagreements about job processes were solved by defining consensus as, "Can you live with it?" and "Will you be able to sleep tonight?" rather than forcing total agreement with each step and task.

- *Disseminating organizational knowledge.* Although the JRPs and JADs produced agreed-upon content, the content's breadth often spanned a range of expert examiner work processes. Everyone agreed that there was no one correct way, but the question was now, "Which right ways should become the standards?" At the organizational level, the steering committee was responsible for making this decision. Similar to the debate that occurred at the JRPs and JADs between the SMEs, the steering committee also had a difficult time agreeing on the best of the "best practices." One particularly troublesome example was the expert examiners' mental model for conducting cause exams. After a lengthy discussion, the steering committee rejected the design team's recommendations. The design team revised the cause model, prototyped it, and then demonstrated it to the steering committee. It was then accepted and included in the CBT.

- Once the organizational knowledge was captured, the question became how to disseminate it. The difficulty with any large-scale project that significantly affects employees' current work processes is that the organizational change timeline often lags behind the project timeline. In other words, many organizations don't prepare (or even inform) their employees of the changes that are occurring until after they are implemented. As part of the change management process, the NASD and DLS determined that an initial communication about CORNERSTONE would help answer questions and address potential concerns about job changes that examiners were hearing about through the company grapevine. CORNERSTONE's *Electronic Brochure* described each of the PSS components, the type of information included in each component, and how the information was obtained. Distributed to all examiners one month before CORNERSTONE's implementation, the Electronic Brochure was successful in alleviating initial concerns about changes to examiners' jobs.

- *Employing a full-time project manager.* Throughout the development effort, both the NASD and DLS had full-time project managers dedicated to tracking the CORNERSTONE project. For a project the size of CORNERSTONE, managing the project administration, logistics, and tasking was no small effort. Therefore, the NASD and DLS project managers had daily contact, tracked "inchstone" progress, and met in person on a monthly basis for status meetings.

However, it wasn't until after the analysis phase that one person assumed the project manager role for both the NASD and DLS. The NASD first realized that there needed to be one dedicated, constant project leader during one of the initial steering committee meetings. The participants on the steering committee came from different backgrounds, jobs, and geographic locations, which often made decision making a painstaking process. Clearly after the first few debates, it became evident that consensus would not be reached as a group and that someone needed the authority to break ties and make decisions.

Although DLS always enlisted a dedicated project manager, the role changed hands three times prior to the design phase. There were different reasons for these changes, including employee turnover and other staff resource constraints. In spite of the lack of continuity, the project made ample progress. While working through CORNERSTONE's design issues, DLS's new project manager emerged as the one responsible for the tremendous coordination and tracking effort required. Throughout the project, DLS's project manager proved to be a steady, level-headed, consistent foundation upon which CORNERSTONE was successfully built.

CORNERSTONE Description and Delivery

Congruent with the recommendations of Senge (1990), Banathy (1992), and Salisbury (1996), CORNERSTONE reflects a systems-level thinking structure applied to HPT. As such, CORNERSTONE employs a wide range of processes, devices, and people, as depicted in the following section.

CORNERSTONE Components

The purpose of CORNERSTONE is to provide integrated tools, information, advice, and training that novice and expert NASD examiners need to perform their jobs. Comprising 21 different components and 10 different types of media, CORNERSTONE represents one of the largest PSSs created to date. The following sections illustrate CORNERSTONE's components:

1. *Electronic Brochure:* This 20-minute informational CD-ROM (programmed using Macromedia Director) serves two purposes. First, it alleviates the anxieties of NASD examiners, who are naturally concerned about the changes CORNERSTONE brings to their jobs. Released prior to the rest of the PSS, this marketing brochure helped abate informational concerns by describing how CORNERSTONE was based on the captured expertise of the NASD's best examiners, incorporates the same types of technology its members were already using, and supports the performance of novices and experienced examiners alike. The brochure also describes the major training and job components of CORNERSTONE, its ease of use, and flexibility. Second, the brochure

now acts as the standard introduction to CORNERSTONE and NASD uses it as a recruiting tool for potential examiners.

2. Self-paced manuals foundations training: This group of eight courses allows novice examiners to master the basic skills and knowledge they need to do their jobs. Primarily procedural, topics include their role at the NASD, product lines, brokerage operations, and SEC rules. This training also includes an introduction to the examination process that acquaints examiners with the mental model experts employ.

3. Electronic performance support system: This EPSS comprises the "heart" of CORNERSTONE. It resides on desktop computers that examiners and supervisors use in the NASD district offices and on laptop computers that examiners use in the field. As such, it provides on-demand, flexible access to training, information, and software tools examiners use to perform their jobs.

4. Computer-based training: Programmed using Microsoft's Visual Basic (VB), this component of the EPSS allows novice examiners to apply the mental models and prerequisite skills they learned in foundations training using cognitive apprenticeship techniques. During initial lessons, examiners complete case studies based on actual examinations. To demonstrate final mastery, examiners complete the Case Study Challenge, a goal-based scenario (Schank & Cleary, 1995) that allows examiners to request information from member firms, interview customers, review audit trails, and determine whether a hypothetical firm is in compliance with securities regulations and procedures. The CBT's modular structure also enables experienced examiners to complete refresher courses or cross-training.

5. Hypertext product information: This Microsoft WinHelp application consists of approximately 150 hypertext pages and provides product information describing the securities industry and its regulations. The user interface of this EPSS component is organized using 10 product categories and questions expert examiners typically ask when they encounter new products, employing whole-to-part sequencing.

6. Automated examination modules (AEM): Also programmed in VB, AEM replaces the cumbersome paper-based forms examiners used to conduct exams. This custom software helps examiners plan their examinations, review and organize the data they collect during an examination, and prepare a rough draft of their examination report. AEM supports the spectrum of examiners, by including an exam coach (for novice examiners) and an AEM coach (for novice PC users). This component of the EPSS also contains integrated spreadsheets and other financial tools that examiners typically employ in an exam. In addition, AEM allows examiners to access examination procedures on-demand.

7. Hypertext reference information: This EPSS component contains off-the-shelf, online documentation describing rules, regulations, and policies.

8. Hypertext help system: This component describes how to use the EPSS.

9. Printed job aids: Novice examiners use these materials to complete the mentoring and on-the-job training components of their training.

10. Mentoring and on-the-job training: To ensure that examiners receive numerous ongoing opportunities to apply what they learn in training to what they do on an examination, examiners complete both a formal mentorship and structured on-the-job training. Mentors are responsible for the day-to-day implementation of CORNERSTONE for their protégés. In addition to answering questions that arise, mentors use the CORNERSTONE training management tool (the student database component of the CBT) to create custom training and testing paths for each novice examiner, enable their tests, review student performance records, change passwords, and create reports.

Mentors also work with examiners' supervisors to schedule on-the-job training activities in which novices accompany more experienced examiners to complete specific examination tasks. This component of CORNERSTONE requires novices to transfer what they learned in the district office to what they do in the field.

11. Instructor-led, problem-based advanced examiners' seminar: This CORNERSTONE component involves a week-long problem-based learning class that builds upon each CORNERSTONE component the examiner has accessed thus far. During this time, examiners work in teams to complete a simulation of two complex examinations. This seminar blends the "hard" technologies embodied in the hypertext product information and automated exam modules with the best that cooperative learning experiences offer: teamwork, group interactions, coaching, modeling, tutoring, and complex feedback.

12. Instructor-led mentor training: The last component of CORNERSTONE consists of a three-day course for mentors based on the completion of role-play exercises. During this time, mentors learn how to interact with their protégés using their paper and software-based mentoring tools.

Models and Techniques

To ensure that the software components would work as expected upon their implementation, the project employed a modified version of Rapid Application Development (RAD) methodology (Martin, 1991). The first two components of this methodology involved collaborative analysis and design as well as iterative prototyping. In JRP and JAD workshops, participants refined system functional requirements and user interface design. DLS, in turn, revised prototypes of the components to reflect the design decisions made during the workshops. These workshops also ensured that examiners would buy into the software applications they had helped design, test, and implement. This technique was crucial in helping reach consensus between the diverse backgrounds of the technical review teams and the steering committee, whose approval was instrumental in CORNERSTONE's ultimate success.

Another technique that DLS employed was the layers of necessity model, created by Wedman and Tessmer (1990), which provides a methodology for "timeboxing" a project. Timeboxing is an alternative description of decisions that performance technologists make when they create interventions (Villachica & Stone, 1998). In using layers of necessity to timebox, instructional designers create one or more layers of design activities that meet the constraints of project resources, which could include time, money, design expertise, and organizational goals.

With a project as large and as complex as CORNERSTONE, it became evident that strict project management controls had to be employed to ensure that all of the project budget wasn't expended during design. The layers of necessity model enabled the NASD and DLS to tailor the amount of analysis and design activities to meet the budget and time constraints. After the first layer of design activities was complete—thereby providing what was absolutely necessary to meet examiners' performance requirements—additional layers were added as the steering committee deemed necessary.

Costs

The CORNERSTONE development effort began in 1994, starting with the self-paced foundations courses. NASD provided SMEs to create course content, and DLS exclusively developed the PSS components. In addition to DLS's costs, there were two other categories that contributed to costs: NASD development costs and capital equipment expenditures. For purposes of simplicity, the costs for CORNERSTONE were grouped into the three categories as depicted in table 3.

Vendor development costs included all the labor costs and expenses involved in creating the CORNERSTONE program. NASD development costs consisted primarily of the labor costs of NASD Steering Committee members, Technical Review Team members, and SMEs as-

Table 3. NASD return-on-investment and payback period calculations.

Assumptions for the financial calculations:

- 15 student training days per year (savings of 50%)
- average burdened examiner daily rate is $250
- average examiner travel cost is $6,000 per student, per year (savings of 33%)

Costs	1994	1995 (Year 1)	1996 (Year 2)	1997 (Year 3)	Total
Vendor development	$800,000	$200,000	$0	$0	
Customer development	$50,000	$0	$0	$0	
Capital equipment	$20,000	$180,000	$180,000	$180,000	
Total costs	$870,000	$380,000	$180,000	$180,000	$1,610,000

Savings	1994	1995 (Year 1)	1996 (Year 2)	1997 (Year 3)	Total
New hires per year		75	100	100	
Student time savings		$281,250	$375,000	$375,000	
Student travel savings		$450,000	$600,000	$600,000	
Total savings		$731,250	$975,000	$975,000	$2,681,250

Calculations	End Result
Return-on-investment	2.5 or 60%
Payback period	1.53 years

signed to the project. In order to support the new technology from a computer infrastructure perspective, the NASD purchased equipment specifically for CORNERSTONE. Overall, the cost to develop and implement CORNERSTONE was $1,610,000.

Data Analysis and Results

Results from CORNERSTONE can be divided into two categories: financial and impact on the NASD. From a data analysis perspective, the NASD identified the type of information it was most interested in tracking. Not all possible savings and benefits were included, however, in the interest of keeping the estimates conservative and believable by the NASD's financial personnel.

Financial Results

The two primary financial calculations that the NASD requested were a return-on-investment (ROI) calculation and the project's payback period. Because the NASD's controller would be the main party interested in these calculations, they needed to be based upon finance principles, rather than strictly training ROI calculations. Therefore, fundamental within the ROI calculation was cumulative cash flow, determined over four years. To determine cumulative cash flow, or savings over four years, deduct the costs from the previous year and current year from the savings from the current year. Continue the calculation for each desired year. To calculate ROI, divide the total cumulative cash flow, or savings, from the total costs. CORNERSTONE's ROI was 2.5, which means for every dollar invested in CORNERSTONE, the return to the NASD was $2.50 in increased examiner efficiency and productivity. In other words, CORNERSTONE's benefits exceeded its costs by 60 percent.

CORNERSTONE's payback period also proved to be an excellent way to determine its worth. Typically, payback period calculations show the expected number of years that it takes to recoup a project's investment. In the case of CORNERSTONE, the calculation was based on actual values, however, rather than expected values. Cumulative cash flow becomes positive between years one and two; therefore, based on the calculation, CORNERSTONE paid for itself after 1.53 years, or somewhere between 1995 and 1996.

CORNERSTONE's Impact on the NASD

Summative evaluation data collected to date indicates that CORNERSTONE has succeeded in closing the targeted performance gaps, as summarized in table 4 (Villachica & Stone, 1998).

Table 4. CornerStone organizational outcomes.

Desired Performance	Evidence
Novice examiners need to master their jobs as quickly as possible.	Preliminary indications show that mastery time will be reduced from 2.5 years to one year, a reduction of 60 percent.
Experienced examiners should remain with their jobs with the NASD for a longer period of time.	Mentors were formally selected and trained. Anecdotal evidence suggests that mentors feel they are recognized and rewarded for their knowledge and extra efforts.
Examiners must keep paced with changes in securities products and regulations.	CornerStone's ability to access timely information has eliminated the time examiners once spent creating and maintaining their own libraries of securities products, examination procedures, and securities regulations.
The decision processes that SMEs use to conduct examinations should be captured and disseminated.	The self-paced print materials, *Introduction to Cycle* and *Introduction to Cause*, teach the mental models that expert examiners use to conduct the respective exams.
Examiner training should adequately prepare them to perform their jobs.	Anecdotal data indicate that examiners who have completed CornerStone training possess the skills and confidence to conduct exams with less intervention from mentors and experienced examiners.
The modules (form-based job aids) that examiners complete when they conduct exams should be current and easy to use.	By reducing the time required to conduct examinations, the NASD saved approximately $2 million annually in reduced employee needs. In addition, the conversion from a print-based system to a digital system substantially reduced administrative costs, including paper reproduction and distribution of regulatory updates and revisions to field examiners. Anecdotal self-report data reveal that AEM users feel the software is helpful, intuitive and easy to navigate.

Although NASD and DLS collected the data both formally and informally, the outcomes of CORNERSTONE not only closed the identified performance gaps, but also improved productivity and increased job satisfaction. Other business benefits from CORNERSTONE include:

- Reduced training delivery costs of 43 percent reduction because of on-demand training.
- Decreased potential that regulatory violations might harm the investing public during the time a novice examiner comes up to speed.
- Provided experienced examiners with new opportunities to advance in their careers. After five years on the job, supervisors can select these individuals as mentors, a role in which they also receive formal training.
- Increased employee satisfaction.
- Increased customer satisfaction by 26 percent (based on results from the NASD's annual member survey).
- Increased novice examiners' knowledge about new products. Prior to CORNERSTONE, novice examiners at times relied on members of the securities firms they investigated to teach them about new products the member was trading. Examiners can now access this information on demand.
- Increased consistency in exam performance and decreased unnecessary district variation in exam processes by providing explicit learning of experts' decision processes.
- Reduced rework required by examiners due to exam reports returned by supervisors, managers, and legal personnel.
- Provided the opportunity for 100 percent of the steering committee and 30 percent of the technical review team to receive promotions.
- Improved appearance of professionalism.

Conclusions and Recommendations

Perhaps the single, most critical factor that ensured CORNERSTONE's overall achievements was its ability to handle dramatic change. During 1996, the NASD experienced tumultuous changes to its upper-level management. A new president was named, who in turn named a new executive support staff. With the new president came goals that were different from the previous president. This could have been disastrous for the NASD's examiners. However, CORNERSTONE's job performance orientation, modularity, and flexibility allowed the new president to achieve her goals while supporting and maintaining examiner performance. Because of the varied organizational distribution of project team members and their corresponding impact on the design, CORNERSTONE could accommodate the changes to senior management, their goals, and to the NASD culture.

Knowledge workers perform their jobs within complex, hierarchical systems. Performance gaps that occur within such systems usually "travel in packs" and interact with each other in complex, indeterminate ways. Addressing specific gaps in isolation usually fails because the inertia of the system itself overcomes isolated attempts to change it. Closing such interacting gaps requires a systemic view of performance and how it should be supported. CORNERSTONE succeeded in closing a variety of interrelated performance gaps because it addressed them systemically. Critical to its success were the strategies it employed to automate manual work processes, make complex skills and knowledge visible, and extend the range of existing EPSS design approaches by integrating them with off-line interventions (Villachica & Stone, 1998).

In contrast, providing technology-based, self-paced training alone would not have closed this performance gap to the same extent as CORNERSTONE. This training-first approach embodies a "subsystem" focus that is inherently incapable of solving systemic performance problems. Providing such training may have slightly reduced time to mastery, but not to the extent CORNERSTONE made possible. Without investigating the system the NASD used to provide training to novices, the full scope of the performance gaps would not have been discovered—or resolved (Stone & Villachica, 1997). The other links of the performance support chain would have remained broken and would likely have instigated other performance problems. The NASD and DLS avoided these problems by following a systematic approach to analysis, design, and development, and was fortunate to have a committed, high-level sponsor and project team members willing to acquire new skill sets. The team's ability to think outside of the training box enabled the NASD and DLS to declare and publicize CORNERSTONE's success.

Questions for Discussion

1. Based on the way the authors described the process of performance analysis in this case, how is it clear that this situation warranted a combination of training and nontraining interventions? Why do you think so?

2. What types of issues would you expect to face when trying to reach consensus on design issues from an audience with widely varied backgrounds and geographic locations? What techniques might you use to overcome these issues?

3. Based on the information you know about the NASD's examiner population, what other types of interventions might you select to close the identified performance gaps? Why would you select them?

4. Which results do you think were most important to the NASD, financial or impact? Why?

5. The NASD and DLS collaborated and worked together extensively throughout this project. What are some of the benefits of extensive collaboration? What are some of the shortcomings?

The Authors

Andrea K. Moore is a project manager and instructional designer for DLS Group, where she specializes in creating award-winning performance support systems for business and industry. She has worked on PSS- and EPSS-related projects in the securities, transportation, high-tech, and banking industries for the last six years. She has also created computer-based training, multimedia, print-based training, instructor-led training, and job aids. As a human factors engineer, Moore has developed numerous prototypes and graphical user interfaces using a variety of packages. A member of both the International Society for Performance Improvement and the Front Range Chapter, she is a frequently published author and recognized presenter. A graduate of Purdue University, Moore's B.S. in industrial engineering has helped her pioneer efficient, easy-to-use computer interfaces for EPSS, multimedia, and CBT applications. Moreover, her M.B.A. background has brought additional rigor, without sacrificing flexibility, to DLS's project management process. Moore can be contacted at the following address: DLS Group, 44 Cook Street, Suite 880, Denver, CO 80206.

Deborah L. Stone is the president of DLS Group and has received 18 professional awards of excellence across the industry for her work in instructional design, technology-based training, and PSSs. One of these PSSs, created for the securities industry, consists of 20 components and employs 12 different media, including multimedia, self-paced manuals, EPSS (CBT, online hypertext reference, and custom software), on-the-job training, formal mentoring, problem-based learning, and instructor-led training. A frequently published author and international presenter, Stone completed her graduate work in instructional technology at San Francisco State University. In addition to ASTD, she is currently active in the International Society for Performance Improvement, a member of its Human Performance Technology faculty, and a frequent presenter at the Interactive Conference. She also serves on the advisory board of the University of Colorado's Graduate Division of Instructional Technology.

References

Banathy, B.H. (1992). *A Systems View of Education: Concepts and Principles for Effective Practice.* Englewood Cliffs, NJ: Educational Technology.

Kulik, C.C., J.A. Kulik, and B.J. Shwalb. (1986). "The Effectiveness of Computer-Based Adult Education: A Meta-Analysis." *Journal of Educational Computing Research, 2*(2), 235-252.

Mager, R., and P. Pipe. (1984). *Analyzing Performance Problems or You Really Oughta Wanna* (2d edition). Belmont, CA: Fearon.

Martin, J. (1991). *Rapid Application Development.* New York: Macmillan.

Rossett, A. (1987). *Training Needs Assessment.* Englewood Cliffs, NJ: Educational Technology.

Rossett, A., and J.A. Gautier-Downes. (1991). *Handbook of Job Aids.* San Diego, CA: Pfieffer.

Rummler, G., and A. Brache. (1995). *Improving Performance* (2d edition). San Francisco: Jossey-Bass.

Salisbury, D.F. (1996). *Five Technologies for Educational Change: Systems Thinking, Systems Design, Quality Science, Change Management, Instructional Technology.* Englewood Cliffs, NJ: Educational Technology.

Senge, P.M. (1990). *The Fifth Discipline: The Art and Practice of the Learning Organization.* New York: Doubleday.

Shank, R.C., and C. Cleary (1995). *Engines for Education.* Hillsdale, NJ: Lawrence Erlbaum Associates.

Stone, D.L., and S.W. Villachica. (1997). "Performance Support for Knowledge Workers." *Performance Improvement, 36*(3), 6-12.

Villachica, S.W. (1996). "Program Reduces Training and Improves Performance." *Multimedia Training Newsletter, 3*(8), 4.

Villachica, S.W., and D.L. Stone. (1998a). "CORNERSTONE: A Case Study of a Large-Scale Performance Support System." In P.J. Dean and D.E. Ripley, editors, *Performance Improvement Interventions: Methods for Organizational Learning.* Washington, DC: International Society for Performance Improvement.

Villachica, S.W., and D.L. Stone. (1998b). "Rapid Application Development for Performance Technology: Five Strategies to Deliver Better Interventions in Less Time." In P.J. Dean and D.E. Ripley, editors, *Performance Improvement Interventions: Methods for Organizational Learning.* Washington, DC: International Society for Performance Improvement.

Wedman, J., and M. Tessmer. (1990). "The 'Layers of Necessity' ID Model." *Performance and Instruction, 29*(4), 1-8.

About the Editors

William J. Rothwell is professor of human resource development (HRD) in the Department of Adult Education, Instructional Systems and Workforce Education and Development, in the College of Education on the University Park Campus of The Pennsylvania State University. In that capacity he directs a graduate program in HRD. He is also director of Penn State's Institute for Research in Training and Development.

Before arriving at Penn State in 1993, he was an assistant vice president and management development director for the 28th largest life insurance company in the United States (of 1,200 companies) and before that, a training director in a state government audit agency. He has worked full-time in human resource management and employee training and development since 1979. He thus combines real-world experience with academic and consulting experience. Rothwell was chairperson of the American Society for Training & Development (ASTD) Publishing Review Committee when the *In Action* series was authorized, and he remains a strong supporter of the concept of providing real-world cases to practitioners and academics.

Rothwell's latest publications include *Mastering the Instructional Design Process* (2d ed., 1998, with H.C. Kazanas), *Beyond Instruction: Comprehensive Program Planning for Business and Education* (1997, with Peter S. Cookson), *Beyond Training and Development: State-of-the-Art Strategies for Enhancing Human Performance* (1996), *The ASTD Models for Human Performance Improvement* (1996), *The Self-Directed On-the-Job Learning Workshop* (1996), *The Just-in-Time Training Assessment Instrument* (1996), *The Just-in-Time Training Administrator's Handbook* (1996), *Developing the High Performance Workplace: Administrator's Handbook* (1996, with David Dubois), and *Developing the High Performance Workplace: Organizational Assessment Instrument* (1996, with David Dubois).

Rothwell has been author, coauthor, editor, or coeditor of numerous other publications, including: *Strategic Human Resource Planning* (1988, with H.C. Kazanas), *Strategic Human Resource Development* (1989, with H.C. Kazanas), *The ASTD Reference Guide to Professional Training and*

Development Roles and Competencies (1989, 2 volumes, with Henry J. Sredl), *The Strategic Planning Workshop* (1989), *The Structured On-the-Job Training Workshop* (1990, 2 volumes), *The Workplace Literacy Primer* (1990, with Dale Brandenburg), *Mastering the Instructional Design Process: A Systematic Approach* (1992, with H.C. Kazanas), *The ASTD Reference Guide to Professional Human Resource Development Roles and Competencies* (1992, 2 volumes, with Henry J. Sredl), *The Employee Selection Workshop* (1992, 2 volumes), *The Employee Discipline Workshop* (1992, 2 volumes), *The Complete AMA Guide to Management Development* (1993, with H. C. Kazanas), *Improving On-the-Job Training* (1994, with H.C. Kazanas), *Human Resource Development: A Strategic Approach* (1994, rev. ed.), *Planning and Managing Human Resources: Strategic Planning for Personnel Management* (1994, rev. ed.), *Effective Succession Planning: Ensuring Leadership Continuity and Building Talent from Within* (1994), *Practicing Organization Development: A Handbook for Consultants* (1995), and *The Emerging Issues in HRD Sourcebook* (1995).

Rothwell earned his undergraduate degree at Illinois State University, completed a master's and all course work for a doctorate in English at the University of Illinois at Urbana-Champaign, earned an M.B.A. with specialized courses in human resource management from Sangamon State University (now the University of Illinois at Springfield), and (in a second doctoral program) completed a Ph.D. in human resource development at the University of Illinois at Urbana-Champaign.

In 1996, Rothwell completed "A 21st Century Vision of Strategic Human Resource Management," an unpublished research report from a project sponsored by the Society for Human Resource Management, the Research Committee of the Society for Human Resource Management, and CCH, Inc.

Accredited for life as a senior professional in human resources (SPHR), he has been a consultant for over 30 Fortune 500 companies, including Motorola, General Motors, and Ford Motor Company (world headquarters). He can be reached at 647 Berkshire Drive, State College, PA 16803; phone: 814.234.6888; fax: 814.235.0528.

David D. Dubois is the president of Dubois & Associates, a consulting firm that specializes in the creation and implementation of competency-based performance improvement systems that support high performance in organizations and competency-based performance management systems. Dubois has numerous years of experience in creating competency-based performance enhancement interventions and human resource management systems, including performance management.

He holds B.S degrees in mathematics and education from Indiana University of Pennsylvania; M.S. degrees in mathematics and education from The American University; a Ph.D. in science education from The American University; and an M.A. in counseling from Virginia Polytechnic Institute and State University.

Dubois is the author of the highly acclaimed and best-selling book, *Competency-Based Performance Improvement: A Strategy for Organizational Change* (1993). He is the author of the *Competency-Based Performance Improvement Organizational Assessment Package* and he is the senior co-author of *Developing the High-Performance Workplace Organizational Assessment Package* (1995 and 1996, respectively). His latest books include *The Executive's Guide to Competency-Based Performance Improvement* and also *The Competency Case Book: Twelve Studies in Competency-Based Performance Improvement* (1996 and 1998, respectively).

Dubois has numerous articles published in internationally refereed professional journals on a wide variety of topics. He has researched, developed, and been author of numerous policy and technical reports, curriculum documents, position papers, evaluation reports, financial reports, and training documents.

Dubois was the 1994-1995 chair of the ASTD Publishing Review Committee; he was a committee member for two years prior to being its chair. He is currently an associate editor for the *International Journal of Training & Development*. He holds membership in ASTD, the International Society for Performance Improvement, American Counseling Association, and the National Career Development Association. Dubois is a licensed professional counselor in the District of Columbia. He has received numerous awards for his accomplishments.

He has experience in consulting, program development, delivering invited presentations, and as a workshop leader with organizations including Federal Express/Roberts Express, Inc.; USDA Graduate School; the Law Firm of Morgan, Brown & Joy; Insep Consuitants (France); Loyola College; Coca-Cola, Inc.; University of Michigan Medical Center; Baker, Hughes, INTEQ; Department of Labor

(NOICC); Knowledge Resources (S. Africa); National Academy for Public Administration; International Quality & Productivity Center, Inc.; International Society for Performance Improvement; American Society for Training & Development; Linkage, Inc.; Lockheed-Idaho, Inc.; the Executive Study Conference; University of Michigan School of Education; Ford Motor Company (world headquarters); Ziff Institute: State University of New York (Albany); and the American Counseling Association. He can be reached at P.O. Box 10340, Rockville, MD 20849-0340; phone: 301.762.5026; fax: 301.762.5026.

About the Series Editor

Jack J. Phillips has more than 27 years of professional experience in human resources and management and has served as training and development manager at two Fortune 500 firms, been president of a regional federal savings bank, and was management professor at a major state university.

In 1992, Phillips founded Performance Resources Organization, an international consulting firm specializing in human resources account-ability programs. Phillips consults with clients in the United States, Canada, England, Belgium, Germany, Sweden, Italy, South Africa, Mexico, Venezuela, Malaysia, Indonesia, Hong Kong, Australia, and Singapore. His clients include Motorola, Andersen Consulting, State Street Bank, UPS, Nortel, Canadian Imperial Bank of Commerce, DHL Worldwide Express, Singapore Airlines, Caltex Pacific, First Union National Bank, Exxon, and Guthrie Healthcare. He has also consulted with several state and federal government agencies in the United States, Canada, Europe, and Asia.

A frequent contributor to management literature, Phillips has authored or edited 20 books including *Return on Investment in Training and Performance Improvement* (1997), *Accountability in Human Resource Management* (1996), *Handbook of Training Evaluation and Measurement Methods* (3d edition, 1997), *Measuring Return on Investment* (vol. 1, 1994; vol. 2, 1997), *Conducting Needs Assessment* (1995), *The Development of a Human Resource Effectiveness Index* (1988), *Recruiting, Training and Retaining New Employees* (1987), and *Improving Supervisors' Effectiveness* (1985), which won an award from the Society for Human Resource Management. Phillips has written more than 100 articles for professional, business, and trade publications.

Phillips has earned undergraduate degrees in electrical engineering, physics, and mathematics from Southern Polytechnic State University and Oglethorpe University; a master's in decision sciences from Georgia State University; and a Ph.D. in human resource management from the University of Alabama. In 1987, he won the Yoder-Heneman

Personnel Creative Application Award from the Society for Human Resource Management. He is an active member of several professional organizations.

Jack Phillips can be reached at Performance Resources Organization, P.O. Box 380637, Birmingham, AL 34238-0637; phone: 205. 678.9700; fax: 205.678.8070.

Other Books Available in the Series

The ASTD *In Action* series examines real-life case studies that show how human resource development (HRD) professionals analyze what worked and what didn't as they crafted on-the-job solutions to address specific aspects of their work. Each book contains 15–25 case studies taken from many types of organizations, large and small, in the United States and abroad. Choose from case study collections on the following topics:

Measuring Return on Investment, Volume 1

Jack J. Phillips, *Editor*

Who's going to support a training program that can't prove itself? This volume shows you case after case of trainers proving that their programs work—in dollar-for-dollar terms. Each of the 18 case studies shows you the best (and sometimes not-so-best) practices from which every trainer can learn. Corporations demand bottom-line results from all branches of their operations, including HRD. This volume hands you the tools—the hows, whys, and how-wells of measuring return-on-investment—to mark that bottom line.

Order Code: PHRO. 1994. 271 pages.

Measuring Return on Investment, Volume 2

Jack J. Phillips, *Editor*

This second volume contains even more case studies focusing on the issue of return-on-investment. Authors reflecting several viewpoints from varied backgrounds examine their diligent pursuit of accountability of training, HRD, and performance improvement programs. The 17 case studies cover a variety of programs from a diverse group of organizations, many of them global in scope. As a group, these case studies add to the growing database of return-on-investment studies and make a unique and significant contribution to the existing literature on the subject.

Order Code: PHRE. 1997. 272 pages.

Designing Training Programs

Donald J. Ford, *Editor*

These days, training techniques must consist of more than setting up flipcharts, handing out manuals, or plugging in audiovisual aids. Organizations are asking instructional designers to create innovative learning systems that use a wide range of methods and media to spark participants' interest and increase retention and use on the job. This volume showcases 18 real-life examples of customized and artful programs that improve learning and staff performance. Computer-based training, distance learning, and on-the-job training are just a few of the many methods used by the contributors to this book.

Order Code: PHTD. 1996. 340 pages.

Transferring Learning to the Workplace

Mary L. Broad, *Editor*

The 17 case studies in this volume cover a wide range of organizational settings. Specifically, the real-life training examples feature dramatic, large-scale knowledge and skill transfer applications that affect overall organizational performance, as well as smaller programs that affect individual employee effectiveness. As more training and HRD professionals struggle to implement learning transfer support activities, this collection of field experiences will be an invaluable source of ideas and advice.

Order Code: PHTL. 1997. 332 pages.

Leading Organizational Change

Elwood F. Holton III, *Editor*

HRD is concerned fundamentally with change, which is traditionally in individual knowledge, skills, and abilities. Today, however, organizations face an ever-increasing rate of change and struggle to manage change processes. HRD professionals have the opportunity to become key players in leading organizational change efforts. Covering a wide range of organizational types, change strategies, interventions, and outcomes, these 14 case studies show that HRD professionals can and should lead change.

Order Code: PHLO. 1997. 260 pages.

Creating the Learning Organization

Karen E. Watkins and Victoria J. Marsick, *Editors*

It's time to take learning organizations out of the think tank and into the real world. This volume of 22 case studies from a cross section of organizations—international and national, industry and service, government and private sector—shows you how to create the learning organization as HRD professionals move beyond theory and into practice, transforming organizations into businesses that perform, think, and learn.

Order Code: PHCL. 1996. 288 pages.

Conducting Needs Assessment

Jack J. Phillips and Elwood F. Holton III, *Editors*

How can you fix performance problems if you don't know what they are? This volume gives you the investigative tools to pinpoint the causes of performance problems—before investing time and money in training. Each of these 17 case studies provides real-world examples of training professionals digging deep to find the causes of performance problems and offers real-world results.

Order Code: PHNA. 1995. 312 pages.

Managing the Small Training Staff

Carol P. McCoy, *Editor*

These 12 case studies explain the challenges and opportunities small training departments face and describe specific success strategies and tactics that proved useful. The book contains practical ideas for action and in-depth examples of what training departments of varying sizes can accomplish. By following the strategies outlined in this book, lone trainers can survive and thrive in today's challenging business environment.

Order Code: PHMS. 1998. 227 pages.

Developing High-Performance Work Teams

Steven D. Jones and Michael M. Beyerlein, *Editors*

Increasingly, companies are experimenting with teams in some area of their organizations. The push for teams comes from market forces that reward efficient companies that are highly responsive to and innovative with changes in their organizations. These 14 case studies present a variety of approaches to implementing high-performance teams in the workplace.

Order Code: PHDH. 1998. 265 pages.

ASTD
1640 King Street
Box 1443
Alexandria, VA 22313-2043
PH 703.683.8100, FX 703.683.8
www.astd.org